Certainty of the Words

Biblical Principles of

Textual Criticism

By Dr. Charles L. Surrett

Surrett Family
Publications

Kings
Mountain, NC

2013

Copyright 2013. All rights reserved.

ISBN 978-0-9789331-1-1

Preface

It was not my original intention to write a second book on the subject of the Greek text of the New Testament, nor do I now anticipate producing yet another. Certainly, there are other significant areas of study that I have pursued, and I desire to put some things in print in those areas. However, the subject of the text of the Scripture keeps coming up for consideration.

It has been my observation that the statements which the Bible has made about itself have been grossly neglected in the study of textual criticism. Most people seem to assume that the "principles" asserted by Westcott and Hort in the production of their Critical Text are factual, and that their conclusions are, then, "scientific." I think that entire system should be challenged in light of numerous Biblical texts about the accuracy and accessibility of the Word of God. Thus, I have felt it necessary to attempt to articulate *Biblical* principles of textual criticism and present them in this book.

Another concern of mine has been that I was ill-prepared to answer the many questions I encountered about the New King James Version. I had not fairly studied the NKJV, and I wanted to be able to evaluate it honestly. That motivated me to do a word-for-word comparison of the NKJV with the 1769 King JamesVersion, which has been the standard English Bible for centuries. I selected the books of Genesis, Romans, and Revelation, to see what differences there were, and to see what the original language lexicons had to say about those differences. Since that study took into account more than 50,000 words of Scripture, I felt it was a fair enough sampling to lead to a reliable conclusion. I was able to confirm, on the basis of Hebrew and Greek exegesis, the decided superiority of the old KJV, when compared with the NKJV. I now believe that I can answer questions about the NKJV with a measure of expertise on the subject.

Whereas many authors who deal with the subject of textual criticism, on either side of the debate, spend much time quoting their "cronies" who agree with them, I have taken a different approach here. The vast majority of the quotations included in this book are from the pens of Critical Text advocates, whose observations have unintentionally strengthened the conclusions made here.

Credit is due to Mr. Mack Swaringen, designer of the book cover, and the artist employed, Mr. Brent Giles, whose combined talents have produced an attractiveness to the book. Gratitude is also expressed to Mr. Doug Stoliker, who assisted with some of the research for Appendix C.

It is my hope that this book will help some who have been persuaded that the Critical Text has a "scholarly" basis to reevaluate that position from a *Scriptural* basis. Regardless of how intelligent the individuals are who espouse a position, the Bible must remain as our only authority for faith and practice.

Charles L. Surrett

Table of Contents

Abbreviations and Terminology 6

Chapter 1: Introduction 7

Chapter 2: Accuracy 12

Chapter 3: Authentication. 23

Chapter 4: Accessibility. 37

Chapter 5: Accomplishment 54

Chapter 6: W-H Principles of Textual Criticism . . 60

Chapter 7: What about the New King James? 72

Chapter 8: Conclusion 79

Appendix A: Comparisons in Genesis 83

Appendix B: Comparisons in Romans 108

Appendix C: Comparisons in Revelation 119

Endnotes 126

Abbreviations Frequently Used

BAG = Bauer, Arndt, and Gingrich Greek Lexicon.

BDB = Brown, Driver, and Briggs Hebrew Lexicon.

CT = Critical Text.

MS = Manuscript (complete or partial Greek text).

MT = Majority Text.

TR = *Textus Receptus*.

TWOT = Theological Wordbook of the Old Testament Hebrew Lexicon.

W-H = Westcott and Hort, editors of Critical Text.

Identification of Textual Terminology

TR Stream of Texts	Critical Stream of Texts
Syrian	Sinaiticus (א)
Antiochian	Vaticanus (B)
Byzantine	Western
Majority	Neutral
Traditional	Alexandrian
Textus Receptus	Critical (Westcott & Hort)
King James Version	Modern English Versions
Based upon over 5,250 manuscripts discovered	Based upon about 400 manuscripts discovered

Chapter 1

Introduction

Perhaps the biggest battle raging today among Bible-believers is over the text of the Scriptures, particularly with regard to the New Testament. People who love God's Word differ on which Greek texts best represent the *autographa*, or original writings of the New Testament. The major choices today are the Critical Text, the Majority Text, and the *Textus Receptus*.

The Critical Text, published in 1881 by Westcott and Hort, claims to use the "oldest and best" Greek manuscripts, and is the basis for nearly all of the modern English translations of the Bible. The Majority Text, emphasizing those readings which are represented by the largest number of manuscripts that have been discovered, was published in 1982 by Hodges and Farstad, and has not yet been translated into English. The *Textus Receptus* is a sub-set of the Majority Text, but was assembled far earlier, by Erasmus. His fourth edition, published in 1527, was translated into the Authorized (King James) Version.

In order to choose one of these positions, the student of God's Word becomes automatically involved in textual criticism, which is simply a means of evaluating the worthiness of Greek texts. The various positions follow certain principles of textual criticism which seem logical to their proponents. However, it seems that current writers do not seem to be motivated to begin with *Bible* principles for these considerations.

Since the Bible, for Baptists, is the *only* authority for faith and practice, it is surprising that this same concept has been so long neglected in the debate over textual criticism. A great principle of hermeneutics (Bible interpretation) is that one must allow Scripture to *interpret* Scripture. Why, then, can one not follow the same concept in textual criticism and allow Scripture to *validate* Scripture? That is, first determine what the Bible has already said about itself, and then choose textual readings which meet those criteria. While many today would lay claim to a *scientific* approach to textual criticism, it seems far more appropriate to use a *Biblical* approach in the choice of Biblical texts. Although he takes a different textual position from that which is advocated here, Michael Harding has properly said:

> "The Scriptures are *self-authenticating* (*emphasis his*) in that they claim divine authority for themselves. . . . Scripture cannot appeal to some higher authority outside itself for authentication. God is the author of Scripture; there is no greater authority to which one may appeal." [1]

Harding then refers to ". . . The Word of God which is self-evidencing, self-attesting, and self-authenticating."[2] This observation seems to reinforce the concept that there must be greater consideration given to *Biblical* principles of textual criticism than has characteristically been done by scholars.

The proliferation of English translations and versions of the Bible is a popular trend that has kept the presses running and the profits increasing for the publishing companies. Taking a market-driven approach, the publishers have promoted their products to be "user-friendly," as if a

Bible version should be selected on the basis of its readability and cover décor, rather than accuracy of translation. Lost in the process is the real issue: which version of the Bible is the best translation of the best Greek and Hebrew texts?

Those who evaluate Greek and Hebrew manuscripts (abbreviated MSS), in order to ascertain the original writings of Scripture are called textual critics. They realize that the basic issue is not one of translations into English (or any other language), but which Hebrew and Greek texts best represent the originals that God inspired.

This is not a new concept, but was recognized by Jerome, who translated the Bible into Latin in the fourth century, AD. In the explanation of his work to Damasus, written in 383, Jerome used words that appear to fit the twenty-first century scenario, particularly if one substitutes the word "English" where "Latin" appears:

> For if we are to pin our faith to the Latin texts, it is for our opponents to tell us which; for there are almost as many forms of texts as there are copies. If, on the other hand, we are to glean the truth from a comparison of many, why not go back to the original Greek and correct the mistakes introduced by inaccurate translators, and the blundering alterations of confident but ignorant critics, and, further, all that has been inserted or changed by copyists more asleep than awake?[3]

The challenge that currently faces believers in God's Word is discerning, not necessarily which versions are *easiest* or *most enjoyable* to read, but rather which version is the most *accurate* rendering of God's original words. The study, then, must begin with selecting the proper Hebrew and Greek manuscripts, in what is called textual criticism.

There are those who boast in their usage of what they consider to be the "scientific" approach, as they evaluate historical data concerning Bible manuscripts. This often results in treating the Bible as if it were any other ancient historical document, rather than acknowledging its Divine origin and preservation.

They use methodology which appears to be subjective, attempting to reconstruct history on the basis of their own interpretations of archaeological discoveries, while using self-made guidelines for those interpretations. A better approach is to allow the Bible to speak for itself, and then select the textual position that takes into account what the Bible says, using Scripture to validate itself. This will result in *Biblical* principles of textual criticism.

There are four main concepts found in the Bible which will help the believer to evaluate the historical evidence of manuscripts in formulating a proper textual position. The Bible teaches its own **accuracy, authentication, accessibility,** and **accomplishment**, so any Bible version that is considered must meet these criteria, to deserve acceptance.

What have we learned in this chapter?

1. We should use Bible principles to evaluate the Bible.

2. Accuracy is more important than readability.

Chapter 2

Accuracy

The accuracy of the Word of God is asserted clearly in Proverbs 22:20-21:

> Have not I written to thee excellent things in counsels and knowledge, That I might make thee know the certainty of the words of truth; that thou mightest answer the words of truth to them that send unto thee?

The Hebrew word קֹשְׁט, which is translated "certainty" in Proverbs 22:21, is rendered "truth" in Psalm 60:4, the only other place where this masculine noun appears in the Old Testament. Its root has the idea of "binding or tying something to something (TWOT)," with the specific application here to "truth (BDB)." Thus, it is not a "loose," unspecific concept that should come from God's words, but rather a clear message that "binds" one by certainty. "Truth," (אֶמֶת) in v 21, is the most frequently-used KJV translation of that Hebrew word, with a form of "true" appearing in 117 of its 127 usages in the Old Testament. It also indicates "firmness," "faithfulness," "reliability," and "sureness (BDB)." Thus, in Proverbs 22:21, the word "certainty" connotes also "truth," and the word "truth" indicates also "certainty." This gives the reader **double confidence** in the accuracy of God's Word, rather than leaving him to "conjecture" and "ambiguity," terms which are used by many textual critics to describe their own conclusions. All of this certainty of the Scriptures, according to the context of Proverbs 22, is to give the reader greater cause to trust in the Lord (v 19). Ambiguity (lack of clarity) and conjecture (guesswork) do not strengthen faith.

In Psalm 111:7, the writer declares that God's commandments are "sure" (אמן). This Hebrew word is in the form of a Niphal participle, whose root idea is "firmness or certainty. . . . The Niphal participle means 'to be faithful, sure, dependable'. . . ."[4] The application of this verse to the subject at hand is to reinforce the concept of the Bible's own accuracy, leaving the reader with a firm certainty that God's Word is dependable.

The accuracy of the Word of God is also indicated in such passages as II Peter 1:19 ("a more sure word"); Psalm 119:128 ("all thy precepts concerning all things"); Matthew 5:18 ("one jot or one tittle"); John 17:17 ("thy word is truth"); II Samuel 7:28 ("thy words be true"); Proverbs 30:5 ("every word of God is pure"); Psalm 12:6 ("The words of the Lord are pure words"); and Psalm 119:160 ("true from the beginning"). In Galatians 3:16, Paul even takes note of the distinction between singular ("seed") and plural ("seeds"), emphasizing the accuracy of the Scriptures, while Romans 3:4 urges man to acknowledge God as true, and every man who contradicts Him as a liar. Psalm 19:8-9 uses various terms to describe the Word of God, and declares that those words are "right," "pure," "clean," and "righteous."

Whereas God does not want His people to look at His Word through eyes of uncertainty, the majority of modern-day textual critics are unsure of the accuracy of their work, as is evidenced by their own statements. The fathers of contemporary textual criticism, Westcott and Hort, said in the explanatory notes included with their Critical Text that they were uncertain of their own accuracy:

But it is at least theoretically possible that the originality of the text thus attained is relative only, and that all existing documents are affected by errors introduced in the early stages of transmission.[5]

Many such statements could be cited from Westcott and Hort's explanatory notes that indicate a lack of certainty in their own conclusions. These Critical Text editors often wrote of "ambiguity," "conjectures," and other such terms that made their "scientific" system appear not to be very scientific! While one may appreciate the honesty of those who admit they are *guessing*, such a position seems to stand in opposition to God's statement of the "certainty of the words."

Individuals who have produced Greek texts patterned after W-H and some of those who have translated from this "family" of Greek texts have also expressed uncertainty about their work.

Erwin Nestle and Kurt Aland produced a text entitled, Novum Testamentum Graece, in 1960. This Greek text was based upon a similar work by Eberhard Nestle, Erwin's father, who had also followed W-H. For those who wonder what confidence Erwin Nestle had in his product, the following quotation should be instructive: "The number of these further readings was increased with successive impressions and important conjectures were also added."[6]

Kurt Aland was involved in the production of another Greek New Testament, this time with the assistance of Matthew Black, Bruce Metzger, and Allen Wikgren, published in 1966. These editors also gave statements that describe the level of confidence they had in their work, as seen in the introduction: ". . . The Greek text was established, the degree of certainty for the reading adopted in the text was estimated. . . ."[7] "It is the intention of the committee from time to time to revise its work in order to take into account new discoveries and fresh evidence."[8] "Square brackets are used to enclose words which are regarded as having dubious textual validity."[9]

> Double square brackets are used to enclose passages which are regarded as later additions to the text, but which are retained because of their evident antiquity and their importance in the textual tradition.[10]

> By means of the letters A,B,C, and D, enclosed within "braces" { } at the beginning of each set of textual variants, the Committee has sought to indicate the relative degree of certainty . . . for the reading adopted as the text. The letter A signifies that the text is virtually certain, while B indicates that there is some degree of doubt. The letter C means that there is considerable degree of doubt . . . while D shows that there is a very high degree of doubt concerning the reading selected for the text.[11]

Surely, such a low level of confidence in the accuracy of the text on the part of those who assembled it would undermine their readers' confidence in God and His Word.

One who prefers the CT said it this way:

> It is impossible to predict with any degree of confidence what may happen in the immediate future

with regard to the text of the New Testament. Additional early witnesses to the text may be discovered. . . . It seems more likely that the future will see refinement of methods. The result may be a text greatly similar to our present one, but by the use of such methods, greater confidence will be placed in the results. . . . We can be assured that the translations based upon the text of Nestle-Aland and the United Bible Societies are based upon readings that give us the basic message of the original authors.[12]

The same author further indicated a lack of "certainty of the words," by making the following observation: "On the basis of solid study and honest concern for the truth, decisions are made, usually with a great deal of confidence."[13] Those who hold this position are satisfied to have the "basic message," and to "usually" have confidence in their Bibles, but that is far less than what God promised in Proverbs 22:20-21.

Even many otherwise-conservative Bible believers, as a result of their loyalty to the Critical Text, are uncertain about the words of Scripture. Kevin T. Bauder says, ". . . We can know what God said, even if we do not have every single word with which He said it."[14] One of Bauder's colleagues, Roy Beacham, referring to scribal copies, said it this way:

> . . . Those copies were dependable and authoritative to the degree that they accurately reflected the autographs. . . . However, those relatively minor changes and variations that did exist in the copies had no substantial effect on the basic truths or teachings

of Scripture.[15]

The TR proponent may respond by asking whether this is materially different from the "concept inspiration" view of theological liberalism. Since we do not have the autographs, how do we know that the copies we have reflect those autographs in *any degree* of accuracy? Without a promise from God to preserve His Word, how can we be sure that what we have today is either "dependable" *or* "authoritative?" How do we know that the variations are "minor," rather than major?

Another writer says that ". . . scholars can assure us that only a small percentage of the original autographs is in question. . . ."[16] While this is an attempt to "assure," it is decidedly contrasted to the *real* assurance God has given us, that we can "know the certainty of the words of truth (Proverbs 22:21)." This same author who finds his "assurance" from the scholars says, "Another illogical assumption of TR/*Majority Text* advocates is the assumption that certainty is identical with truth."[17] Since it has already been noted earlier in this chapter that the Hebrew words for "certainty" and "truth" in Proverbs 22:21 provide a **double assurance** of accuracy, it is not an "illogical assumption," when the information comes directly from God!

While not a proponent of the *Textus Receptus* position himself, Rolland McCune, on the subject of ecclesiastical separation, made the following statements about the influences of neo-orthodox thought upon the new evangelical view of Scriptures:

. . . (Barthian existentialism) rejects the inherent and

qualitative revelatory authority of the *text* of Scripture (*emphasis his*). . . . Some new evangelicals have gravitated to Barth's view. According to them, . . . it does not matter if there is an infallible Bible or not.[18]

Thus, it is the new evangelical/neo-orthodox view of the Bible that results in a lack of confidence in the written text of the Scriptures. Such a position should not be tolerated by fundamentalist Baptists!

Baptists, throughout their history, have expressed confidence in the accuracy of their Bibles. This is clearly seen by a perusal of doctrinal statements by Baptists and their theological predecessors over the centuries. *Baptist Confessions of Faith*, by William L. Lumpkin, records the confessions of faith of many in that great heritage who felt *certain* that they had accurate Bibles. It is interesting to note that all of those referenced here preceded the publication of Westcott and Hort's work, and it was not uncommon for early Baptists to confidently cite I John 5:7, which the Critical Text omits, as proof of the Trinity.

In 1580, a Mennonite confession composed by John de Rhys and Lubbert Gerrits entitled, "A Brief Confession of the Principal Articles of the Christian Faith," included this statement: "This one God in sacred Scripture is revealed and distinguished into (a) Father, Son and Holy Spirit (b) There are three (and yet) only one God."[19] The footnote for "(b)" cites "John 5:7" as the source, but this is evidently a misprint, as they no doubt intended to cite I John 5:7.

In "A True Confession," published by English Separate Baptists in 1596, the second paragraph states: "And that in this Godhead there bee three distinct persons coeternall, coequall, & coessentiall, being every one of the one & the same God . . . ."[20] Interestingly, they footnote I John 5:7 as one of the proof-texts for this doctrine of the Trinity. Thus, prior to the publication of the KJV, this was accepted by Baptists as part of God's Word.

Thomas Helwys, in 1611, published "A Declaration of Faith of English People Remaining in Amsterdam in Holland." This begins with the assertion,

> That there are THREE which beare record in heaven, the FATHER, the WORD, and the SPIRIT; and these THREE are one GOD, in all equalitie, I Jno. 5:7. . . .[21]

Thus, at about the time of the publication of the KJV in England, I John 5:7 was already accepted by these early Baptists living in Holland.

In 1612-14, the English and Dutch versions of "Propositions and Conclusions concerning True Christian Religion" were published. This states, "That there are three which bear record in heaven, the Father, the Word, and the Holy Spirit; and that these three are one in testimony. . . ."[22] Although the reference is not given, this is virtually a quote of I John 5:7.

The Dordrecht Confession of Faith (1632), which Lumpkin says was ". . . the most influential of all Mennonite confessions. . . ,"[23] in Article V, states:

> . . . Christ, before His ascension, established and instituted His New Testament and left it to His followers, to be and remain an everlasting testament, which He confirmed and sealed with His own precious blood; and which He has so highly commended to them, that neither man or angels may change it, neither take therefrom nor add thereto.[24]

Thus, it appears that they had confidence that the New Testament had remained unchanged until 1632.

In 1677, the second London Confession of Faith said:

> The Old Testament in *Hebrew*, (which was the Native language of the people of God of old) and the New Testament in *Greek*, (which at the time of the writing of it was most generally known to the Nations) [*end of parenthesis not included in the original, but supplied by this author*] being immediately inspired by God, and by his singular care and Providence kept pure in all Ages, are therefore authentical; so as in all controversies of Religion, the Church is finally to appeal unto them.[25]

These early believers were convinced that they had a Greek text that had been preserved "pure" by God throughout church history, and this confidence provided a basis for making the Scriptures their final authority in deciding controversies. Believing that the Greek text has been kept pure, this confession of faith cites I John 5:7 as proof of the Trinity.[26]

The "Orthodox Creed," in 1678, also cited I John 5:7 as a proof of the Trinity.[27] Those Baptists had confidence in their King James Bibles, as is seen from the following:

And by the holy scriptures we understand, the canonical books of the old and new testament, as they are now translated into our English mother-tongue, of which there hath never been any doubt of their verity, and authority, in the protestant churches of Christ to this day.[28]

The Philadelphia Confession of Faith (1742), patterned after the Second London Confession of Faith of 1689, also cited I John 5:7 as proof of the Trinity.[29]

The New Hampshire Confession of Faith, published in 1833, stated that the Bible is a ". . . perfect treasure of heavenly instruction; that it has . . . truth, without any mixture of error. . . ."[30] To which Bible were they referring? At that point in history, the Critical Text had not yet been assembled. This certainty is typical of those who believed and loved the Bible before the "guesswork" of textual critics came into play!

In all of the above-cited statements of faith, the early Baptists seemed convinced that their Bibles were accurate. Their Bibles included I John 5:7 *before* and *after* it was printed in the KJV, and long before that same passage was omitted from the Critical Text. Were all of these early believers deluded, defending their doctrinal view of the Trinity with a "spurious" passage that should not have been a part of their Bibles? Apparently, this is what the modern textual critics would have Bible-believers today to think, but such thoughts further erode the "certainty of the words of truth." Bible-believers today should give more credence to the historic Baptist concept of the accuracy of the Scriptures than to the new evangelical/neo-orthodox uncertainty that has raised its ugly head in this debate.

What have we learned in this chapter?

1. Critical Text advocates are uncertain of the text of Scripture.

2. Baptists have historically had confidence in the text of Scripture.

3. Early Baptists included I John 5:7 in their Bibles.

Chapter 3

Authentication

A second Biblical principle of textual criticism is authentication. By that is meant the approval of Bible-practicing local churches throughout the ages.

I Timothy 3:15 describes the local church as the "pillar and ground of the truth." Appearing in one of the Pastoral epistles, this has immediate application to the local church. Since the church is seen to be the "pillar and ground of the truth," these terms deserve further analysis. "Pillar" (στυλος) is from a word which was literally a "support or carrier."[31] It is used metaphorically in Galatians 2:9 to refer to spiritual leaders as "pillars." This same metaphorical use appears in I Timothy 3:15, with the exception that the "pillar" there is the local church itself, not just a few leaders. The indication is that the local church supports and carries God's truth. Thayer's Lexicon says this word " . . . is used of persons to whose eminence and strength the stability and authority of any institution or organization are due. . . ."[32] In this passage, then, the local church would provide that eminence and strength, ensuring the stability and authority of the truth. Of course, the church is not the *source* of that stability, but is merely the *instrument* of its support.

The word translated "ground" is the Greek word εδραιωμα, of which Kittel says,

> A Church is established which protects and defends the truth against the confusion of myths. . . . It gives the faith and thinking of individuals a sure ground in confession (cf 3:16 etc.). No longer God alone, but

also the Church of God, now guarantees the permanence of the (*alethia*).[33]

The teaching of this passage seems to be that God gave to the local church the responsibility to support, carry, protect, and maintain the accuracy and the authority of the truth. Discussing I Timothy 3:15 in relation to the primacy of the local church, McCune says, "To that institution has been committed the fate of revealed truth in this dispensation."[34] The local church, then, becomes the instrument of God's preservation of His Word.

Another key passage to be considered is Jude 3:

> Beloved, when I gave all diligence to write unto you of the common salvation, it was needful for me to write unto you, and exhort *you* that ye should earnestly contend for the faith which was once delivered unto the saints.

Jude's Epistle, which is a companion to II Peter, warns about creeping apostasy and challenges believers within the local church to guard against it. In this struggle, believers are to depend upon the God who is "able to keep you from falling (v 24)." Thus, the God who preserves believers is about to commission them to be active in the preservation of His Word.

The Greek word here rendered "contend" is from επαγωνιζομαι, which is summarized by the Theological Dictionary of the New Testament as encompassing the ideas of full exertion, rigid discipline, facing opposition (perhaps even martyrdom), and the responsibility that believers have to help others. As a present-tense infinitive, the challenge here is to continuation, despite hardships, for the benefit of others. The term "faith" is πιστις, which signifies, in this instance, the doctrine handed down by the church. "Once" is απαξ, used of the death of Christ (Hebrews 9:26-28; I Peter 3:18) and of man (Hebrews 9:27). The sense of this word is "once for all," indicating something which cannot be repeated. "Delivered" is an aorist passive participle, which speaks of something that has taken place at some point in the past. It appears that, once each book of the Bible was written, it was completed for all time, and should not be considered "fluid," changing with future discoveries. There is nothing in the original language that would lead one to conclude that this "faith" would be corrupted, inaccurate, or incomplete. A corrupted "faith" would not be worth fighting for!

In II Peter 3:2, believers are instructed to be "mindful of the words" of both the Old and New Testaments. The Old Testament, of course, is referenced by the "prophets," and the New is indicated by the "apostles." It is the *words* (ρημα) of these Godly men of which believers should be "mindful." Clearly, it was not just a generic *message* that was to dominate their thinking, but the very *words* that embodied that message.

Verse sixteen of II Peter 3 says that there were individuals who would "wrest" the Scriptures, using στρεβλοω, which signifies to "twist" or "pervert." This warning is still further evidence that the believers were to guard the words of Scripture carefully.

The local church pastor was to be "holding fast the faithful word (Titus 1:9)." At the same time, deacons were to be "holding the mystery of the faith in a pure conscience

(I Timothy 3:9)." The congregation at Philippi was expected to be "holding forth the word of life (Philippians 2:16)," while the Corinthians were told to "keep the ordinances (I Corinthians 11:2)." The term "ordinances" is παραδοσις, which Thayer says is "*a giving over which is done by word of mouth* or *in writing*, i.e. tradition by instruction, narrative, precept, etc." Therefore, the Corinthian believers were to continue the transmission of those words into the future, and the obvious implication is that other local churches were to continue such vigilance.

Thus, the truth should be found in the possession of the majority of Bible-believing local churches throughout this Dispensation. This argues against the theory that the Scriptures were lost to the general public for centuries, which is a basic premise of modern textual criticism. The above-cited doctrinal statements of historic Baptistic groups give some insight into the textual position of sound local churches in the sixteenth century and later. There seems to be little doubt that prior to then, in the Middle Ages, the textual stream from which the *Textus Receptus* is derived had clear dominance in local church use, as is asserted by textual critics of all persuasions. Erwin Nestle, who published a derivative form of the Critical Text, points this out:

> . . . The so-called Koine, i.e. the text-rescension which in Antioch and later in Constantinople attained general circulation (the so-called Byzantine or Imperial Text). . . . as well by the mass of later MSS. Since Erasmus used such late MSS for his edition, we meet this type of text in general in the Textus Receptus. . . .[35]

With the dominance of the TR-type texts clearly

established so far back in history, the debate continues over the earliest period of church history, as many have attempted to discern the prevalent text of the first four centuries, AD.

Unfortunately, the evidence is sparse and knowledge of that period is sketchy. Although some have made dogmatic statements to the effect that the early church fathers did not have the "Syrian," "Byzantine," or TR-type text,[36] it must be admitted that this is simply an argument from *silence*. That is, it would be foolish to assume that archaeologists have found everything that ever existed in those early centuries. While the two main manuscripts from which Westcott and Hort produced their Critical Text came from the fourth century, there is little corroboration of those manuscripts from that time frame, and certainly no *proof* that the other text-type did *not* exist. These two manuscripts (*Sinaiticus* and *Vaticanus*), which differ considerably even from each other, give no evidence of continual use through the centuries, but were discovered about fourteen hundred years later and incorporated into that which became known as the Critical Text, as its foundational documents.

Since the Byzantine empire originally included the area of Biblical Asia Minor, it can be seen that almost all of the New Testament autographs were written to individuals or local churches in that area. Mark and Romans are exceptions, but the other twenty-five New Testament books were either certainly or probably written to people in the area that was part of the Byzantine empire from its beginning. None of the autographs were addressed to residents of Egypt, so it seems reasonable that Byzantine-type manuscripts, of which the TR is a "stream," would tend to have a greater claim for authenticity than do those found in Egypt.

It is common for Bible translations and commentaries to refer to the "oldest and best" texts, as if the *age* of a manuscript automatically proves its *accuracy*. In his commentary after a note on Mark 16:8, A. T. Robertson says: "At this point Aleph and B, the two oldest and best Greek manuscripts of the New Testament, stop with this verse."[37] The <u>New International Version</u>, after Mark 16:8, includes the following statement in brackets: "The two most reliable early manuscripts do not have Mark 16:9-20."[38] But such statements are misleading. "Oldest" and "best" are both superlative terms, doubtless intended to be used in contrast to the "Byzantine," or TR-type texts. The term "oldest" is used to refer to those manuscripts that are the oldest ones *that have been discovered*. It does not mean that there were no manuscripts produced earlier in history, but merely that archaeologists have not yet found them. As a matter of fact, more recent discoveries have forced a CT advocate to note that the last verses of Mark 16 ". . . appear in the earliest versions, probably translated before the end of the second century."[39] Thus, the fourth-century manuscripts used to provide support for the CT may not, after all, be the "oldest." The term "best" is a subjective usage which reflects the prejudices of the user. It would be more historically accurate, when referring to the *Sinaiticus* and *Vaticanus* manuscripts, to speak of them as the "oldest found and least used" of the texts that have been discovered. This terminology more accurately compares those manuscripts to the TR-type texts.

However, the Byzantine-type manuscripts should not be taken lightly, as far as their antiquity goes. One Critical Text follower, Donald Brake, refers in a footnote to a master's thesis by Matthew Williams, presented to

Multnomah Biblical Seminary in 2009, saying, "It is interesting to note that a recent master's thesis found more than thirty unique Byzantine readings in the Gospel of Mark in *Codex Sinaiticus*."[40] Brake adds this observation: "Papyri support evidence that distinctive Byzantine readings were not created in the fourth century but were in existence before the end of the second century, and therefore Byzantine readings merit consideration." [41]

In fact, the writings of the church fathers are sometimes cited to assert that they had no access to the texts that later produced the TR-type stream. However, the writings of the church fathers are not even close to being exactly known today. The following quotes, taken from *The Ante-Nicene Fathers* (referring to those Christians who wrote prior to the Council of Nicea in 325 AD), edited by Alexander Roberts and James Donaldson, explain that there is much room for doubt about the actual writings of the church fathers. Regarding the accuracy of the manuscript of Clement: ". . . There are many slight . . . gaps in the MS, and one whole leaf is supposed to have been lost towards the close."[42] Concerning further inaccuracies in Clement's writing: "The translation is doubtful."[43] "The meaning is here very doubtful."[44] "The text here seems to be corrupt."[45] "The reading is doubtful. . . ."[46] "The MS. is here slightly torn, and we are left to conjecture."[47] Concerning uncertainties in the writings of Mathetes to Dionetus: "The text is here corrupt."[48] "The text is here uncertain, and the sense obscure."[49] "The text is here very doubtful."[50] "A considerable gap here occurs in the MSS."[51] "The sense is here very obscure."[52] "The reading and sense are doubtful."[53] Again, "Both the text and rendering are here somewhat doubtful. . . ."[54]   The editor further declares, "The MS. is here defective."[55]

Many other similar citations could be noted, but with such doubtful renderings of these and other of the Ante-Nicene fathers, it causes the reader to wonder if there should be some textual criticism done on *their* writings, before they can be authoritatively quoted as *not* having access to the TR-type texts!

It is also interesting that Edward Miller's assessment of the writings of the Ante-Nicene fathers uncovered documents that appear to argue against the "conventional wisdom" of the textual critics. In a meticulous way, Miller catalogued his findings:

> Accordingly, I made a toilsome examination for myself of the Fathers before St. Chrysostom, or as I defined them in order to draw a self-acting line, of those who died before 400 A.D., with the result that the Traditional Text is found to stand in the general proportion of 3:2 against other variations, and in a much higher proportion upon thirty test passages. Afterwards, not being satisfied with resting the basis of my argument upon one scrutiny, I went again through the writings of the seventy-six Fathers concerned, . . . besides others who yielded no evidence, and I found that although several more instances were consequently entered in my notebook, the general results remained almost the same. . . . I claim, not only that my attempts have been honest and fair even to self-abnegation, but that the general results which are much more than is required by my argument, . . . abundantly establish the antiquity of

the Traditional Text, by proving the superior acceptance of it during the period at stake to that of any other. Indeed, these examinations have seemed to me . . . to carry back the Traditional Text satisfactorily to the first age. . . .[56]

It has also been noted that the Old Latin translations (which preceded Jerome's Vulgate) reveal that ". . . readings in the European manuscripts are closer to the Byzantine text-type (*emphasis in the original*).[57]

With this information available, why should today's Bible-believers bow at the altar of the modern critics, who make reckless charges about the antiquity of the TR-type texts?

There is evidence in two of the earliest-known translations of the Scripture that some Greek manuscripts existed during the fourth century (and probably even earlier) which contained passages that were omitted in the manuscripts upon which the Critical Text was later based. These two early translations are the Latin *Vulgate* and the Syriac *Peshitta*.

Jerome, in 383 AD, began a Latin translation called the Vulgate, and it included the same twenty-seven books of the New Testament which we now accept. Jerome's translation also included the seven Apocryphal books that the Roman Catholic Church calls "Deutero-canonical." However, this is explained by a Roman Catholic source which says,

> St. Jerome considered the seven Deutero-Canonical books to be NOT inspired by God, but he was

commissioned by Pope Damasus to translate all 73 books into Latin.[58]

It is also noteworthy that Jerome included Mark 16:9-20 and John 7:53-8:11,[59] which are omitted in modern versions by those who say those passages came from a "recent" text. Jerome explained that he was using Greek manuscripts that he considered to be the oldest. In his letter to Damasus, Jerome said:

> I therefore promise in this short Preface the four Gospels only, which are to be taken in the following order, Matthew, Mark, Luke, John, as they have been revised by a comparison of the Greek manuscripts. Only early ones have been used.[60]

Since Jerome lived at about the time that the *Sinaiticus* and *Vaticanus* manuscripts were written, it is of great interest that he did not use those "recent" manuscripts, but only "early" ones. He specifically rejected the textual position of Lucian,[61] which serves as a refutation of the notion that the Byzantine-type readings came as a result of a "Lucianic recension." Regarding the age of the Greek manuscripts used by Jerome, one scholar has observed:

> The Latin Vulgate, therefore, is by no means to be neglected by the biblical critic; and since the anti-Hieronymian Latin translation are (sic) unquestionably of great antiquity, both lead us to discovery of the readings in very ancient Greek manuscripts, which existed prior to the date of any now extant.[62]

It appears that Jerome used Greek texts that predated the *Sinaiticus* and *Vaticanus* texts, which were produced in his day. This is important, in light of the concept assumed by modern scholars that the "Byzantine-type" Greek text of the New Testament *did not exist* in the earliest centuries of church history.

While many have asserted that Jerome reflects a "Western" textual family, CT proponent Kurt Aland refutes this idea and states that in his revision of the Old Latin versions, ". . . the consensus today favors the view that Jerome used a contemporary manuscript of the early Koine type, (the precursor, according to Aland, to the Byzantine text-type)."[63]

If Byzantine-type texts did not exist in the earliest centuries of church history, then one would wonder how the ancient Syriac *Peshitta*, which some have dated as early as the second century,[64] and the Latin translation by Jerome both contained the passage in Mark 16 that modern versions omit. Of course, neither the *Vulgate* nor the *Peshitta* agree completely with the TR-type Greek texts. Nevertheless, it must be that these translations were made from ancient Greek manuscripts which have not yet been discovered -- manuscripts that are part of the tradition called "Byzantine," which ultimately resulted in the *Textus Receptus*, from which the King James Version of the Bible was translated.

There also appears to be evidence that the disputed Trinitarian statement in I John 5:7 (the so-called "Johannine Comma") has the support of very ancient Greek manuscripts. The *Codex Fuldensis*, which is dated in the middle of the sixth century, published a prologue to the canonical epistles, claimed to be written by Jerome, that contained these words:

> Just as these are properly understood and so translated faithfully . . . especially in that text where

we read the unity of the trinity is placed in the first letter of John, where much error has occurred at the hands of unfaithful translators contrary to the word of faith, who have kept just the three words water, blood and spirit in this edition omitting mention of Father, Word and Spirit in which especially the catholic faith is strengthened and the unity of substance of Father, Son and Holy Spirit is attested.[65]

While some critics may question whether Jerome actually wrote these words in the fourth century (and there is no way to certainly know whether this is authentically from Jerome or not), it is still clear that, at least sometime before 550 AD, there were allegations that some had heretically omitted this passage from their Greek texts.

Another evidence for the early appearance of the disputed passage in I John is given (in sarcastic terms) by one who attempts to discredit the passage, but acknowledges its early usage:

> Believed to be as old as the Italian, but less reputable, is the *Spanish text-type*, represented by *cav* and *tol*. Jerome himself is said to have supervised the work of the first Spanish scribes to copy the Vulgate (398), but by the time of our earliest manuscripts the type had developed many peculiarities (some of them perhaps under the influence of the Priscillians, who for instance produced the "three heavenly witnesses" text of 1 John 5:7-8).[66]

This quotation comes from one who is obviously skeptical of the passage under consideration, calling the translation in which it is found to be "less reputable," containing "many peculiarities," yet he acknowledges that the reading existed "by the time of our earliest manuscripts." He thus takes information that other critical text proponents deny (that the reading is early in origin), and tries to explain away these facts with sarcasm. The student of God's Word should take careful note of the *facts*, rather than just a modern writer's *interpretation* of the facts.

In light of the scant evidence that has been discovered about the first four centuries, it cannot be honestly affirmed that the TR-type texts *did not exist* during that period. There is no evidence to prove that the later dominance of those texts represented a *change* in the practice of good local churches. Therefore, in keeping with the clear evidence from the Middle Ages and onward, it appears that local churches throughout history have endorsed a stream of texts that later produced the *Textus Receptus* and its classic translation into English, the King James Version. Thus, this textual position seems best to fit the Biblical test of authentication, as being approved by Bible-believing local churches.

What have we learned in this chapter?

1. God wants local churches to be preserving agents of His Word.

2. Our knowledge of the earliest centuries is very limited.

3. Local churches through history have endorsed the TR-type text.

Chapter 4

Accessibility

A third Biblical principle that is helpful in the evaluation of manuscripts and versions is the matter of accessibility. That is, God has not hidden His Word from man, but has preserved it and made it available to every generation of man since the time of its writing. The key verse for this is Isaiah 59:21:

> As for me, this *is* my covenant with them, saith the LORD; My spirit that *is* upon thee, and my words which I have put in thy mouth, shall not depart out of thy mouth, nor out of the mouth of thy seed, nor out of the mouth of thy seed's seed, saith the LORD, from henceforth and for ever.

Some have objected to the use of this verse to demonstrate the preservation of God's Word, because it appears in an eschatological context. However, regardless of the subject matter, this is a promise for God's Word to be accessible to every succeeding generation. There is no reason to suppose that God would preserve those portions of His Word that predict the future and allow other portions to be lost, since "All scripture is given by inspiration of God (II Timothy 3:16). . . ."

One Critical Text proponent says, ". . . the Bible never speaks of Spirit supervision apart from the original authors and autographs. . . ."[67] Perhaps he should take note of Isaiah 59:21, which speaks both of God's Spirit and His words, promising that the words would be accessible to each succeeding generation.

Isaiah 59:21 uses the plural, "words," to describe that which will be preserved forever. It is not a *singular* "word," which is sometimes used to refer to a general thought, but is the *plural*, which emphasizes the *words* which embody that message. Thus, it is an indication of greater precision than merely the general idea being preserved. The very "words" that are used to express that content are to be preserved. This Hebrew term (דבר) is used 1,439 times in the Old Testament, and in well over half the usages, the KJV renders it, "word," or "words." The reference to Isaiah's "seed," and his "seed's seed" describes a multi-generational process of access to God's Word that would continue "from henceforth and for ever." It therefore follows that, when evaluating Bible manuscripts, one must place great credence in those texts which are seen to have been available to believers throughout the centuries (and generations) of church history.

Another passage that indicates preservation and accessibility is Deuteronomy 29:29: "The secret *things belong* unto the LORD our God: but those *things which are* revealed *belong* unto us and to our children for ever, that *we* may do all the words of this law." "Revealed" (נגלה) is a Niphal participle. The participle indicates unbroken continuity, describing a continual state, whereas the Niphal stem is passive. In this verse, the idea is that these things are continually being disclosed or uncovered, and that this process will continue for each succeeding generation, in unbroken continuity. This accessibility will make possible the obedience that this verse indicates.

A similar concept is seen in Deuteronomy 30:11-14:

For this commandment which I command thee this day, it *is* not hidden from thee, neither *is* it far off. It *is* not in heaven, that thou shouldest say, Who shall go up for us to heaven, and bring it unto us, that we may hear it, and do it? Neither *is* it beyond the sea, that thou shouldest say, Who shall go over the sea for us, and bring it unto us, that we may hear it, and do it? But the word *is* very nigh unto thee, in thy mouth, and in thy heart, that thou mayest do it.

In this passage, the "commandment" is the Hebrew word מצוה, *mitzvah*, which appears 181 times in the Old Testament, and it is used for the Ten Commandments in Exodus 24:12. The *Theological Wordbook of the Old Testament*, in its article on this word, notes:

> God clearly reveals his commandments in order that they may be available to all the people. No one has to spend a lifetime in search of them (Deut 30:11). They are right at hand.[68]

As Isaiah 59:21 promised that God's Word would be "in the mouth" of every generation, so in this passage God's Word is "in the mouth" of believers, again indicating accessibility.

This promise is reiterated in the New Testament, as Romans 10:8 quotes Deuteronomy 30:14 to extend the concept of accessibility to include, not only the Old Testament Law, but also the New Testament Gospel, with these words: "But what saith it? The word is nigh thee, *even* in thy mouth, and in thy heart: that is, the word of faith, which we preach. . . ." It does no injustice to the tenor of these Scriptures to conclude that both the Old Testament and the New will be available to believers for all generations to come.

The concept of God's Word being in man's "mouth" has been noted in Isaiah 59:21, Deuteronomy 30:14, and Romans 10:8. This same terminology is often used to indicate the accessibility and ultimate internalization of God's Word by man. This can be seen in Numbers 23:12; Deuteronomy 18:18; Joshua 1:8; Psalm 40:3; Isaiah 51:16; Jeremiah 1:9; and Malachi 2:6.

In addition, God's Word is to be in man's "heart," no doubt also indicating its accessibility, as seen from the terminology in Deuteronomy 6:6; 11:18; Psalm 37:31; 119:11; Luke 2:51; Romans 10:8; and Hebrews 8:10; 10:16.

While most Bible-believers acknowledge God's inspiration of the original writings, some fail to see that He has preserved His Word through accurate copies. One instance of this is seen in Deuteronomy 17:18-19, where these instructions are given regarding Israel's then-future king:

> And it shall be, when he sitteth upon the throne of his kingdom, that he shall write him a copy of this law in a book out of *that which is* before the priests the Levites: And it shall be with him, and he shall read therein all the days of his life: that he may learn to fear the LORD his God, to keep all the words of this law and these statutes, to do them.

In verse nineteen the king is instructed to daily read the *copy* that was made, so that he could keep "all the words" of the original. God's expectation is obviously that the copy would be accurate, and that the original words would thereby be preserved.

However, regarding the process of copying, Harding says, "The Scriptures recognize the vital distinction between what the original writer wrote and the subsequent copies or translations made by others...." [69]

Harding cites Deuteronomy 17:18 as evidence of the above-mentioned "distinction." But the following verse seems to validate the copy, by instructing the king to read "therein," and then to "... keep all the words of this law and these statutes...." This sounds as if God expects the copy to include the totality (meaning of the Hebrew prefix) of His words. While it is certainly possible that humans could err in making copies (and history has proven this to have been the case), it should also be acknowledged that God is capable of superintending the process in such a way that "all the words" of the originals remain intact for believers to access. The reliable copies were accessible to and used by the local churches throughout their history, and were so used with the confidence that they were true to the originals. To conclude that the result was nothing but error-filled copies is to deny God's part in preserving His Word.

Revealing a low view of Scripture by applying inspiration and preservation only to its "religious purpose," Augustus Hopkins Strong nevertheless makes the following observations:

> Since we have shown that God has made a revelation of himself to man, we may reasonably presume that he will not trust this revelation wholly to human tradition and misrepresentation, but will also provide a record of it essentially trustworthy and sufficient; in other words, that the same Spirit who originally communicated the truth will preside over its publication, so far as is needed to accomplish its religious purpose.[70]

> . . . We shall reasonably presume that he will preserve the record of his revelations in written and accessible documents, handed down from those to whom these revelations were first communicated, and we may expect that these documents will be kept sufficiently correct and trustworthy to accomplish their religious purpose. . . .[71]

Even though Strong adds the subjective disclaimer, "to accomplish its religious purpose," he does allow for the Holy Spirit to "preside over its publication," resulting in "written and accessible documents," which "will be kept sufficiently correct and trustworthy."

A more conservative writer has noted that,

> The new evangelical argument also creates an ambivalence to authority within the Bible itself. Some verses have *no* divine authority because they contain error. . . . The selective process creates a "canon within the canon," and one is forced to weed through the Scripture searching for truth in the midst of error hoping to find the genuine canon. . . . Furthermore, the argument shifts the real authority to

the human mind and away from the Bible's own testimony concerning its origin, nature, and authority (2Tim 3:16-17; 2 Pet 1:21; et al.). Intellectual autonomy is the scarlet sin of theologians and philosophers.[72]

This is an excellent analysis, critiquing a wrong view of Scripture, but why could the same statement not apply to the concept of the *preservation* of Scripture?

The Biblical statements concerning the preservation and accessibility of God's Word would seem to rule out the modern-day Critical Text and cast an air of suspicion upon the translations that are based upon it and its derivatives. The basic position of the W-H theory of textual transmission involves the fact that their principle body of texts was hidden from the public for about fourteen centuries of history. The early manuscripts to which Westcott and Hort gave the greatest credence (*Sinaiticus* and *Vaticanus*) were not available for general use from the fourth century until the nineteenth. If these "oldest and least used" manuscripts were to be given such priority it would, of course, deny that God's Word has been available for every generation of mankind.

Some opponents of Biblical preservation for every generation have referred to the day when the Torah was found in the Temple (during the reign of Josiah), as evidence that the written Word of God has not always been accessible. II Kings 22:8ff and II Chronicles 34:14ff record this event. Since Hilkiah "found" the Torah in the Temple, this is assumed to refute the concept of preservation and accessibility. The logic is that, since it was "found," it must have been "lost" to mankind prior to that. W. Edward Glenny writes:

The Old Testament text was not even preserved publicly throughout Israel's history. King Manasseh must have tried to destroy the Book of the Law, and it was found again in the house of the Lord during the reign of Josiah. Apparently one of the priests had hidden a copy there when Manasseh tried to destroy it (2 Kgs. 22:8-20). Thus, for many years (long enough for it to be forgotten) the only copy of God's Word that existed was hidden in the Temple and not accessible to God's people.[73]

The preceding contexts of II Kings 22 and II Chronicles 34 reveal that the people of Judah apparently had access to the Word of God in the previous generations. Going back to Hezekiah's reign, which began approximately seventy-five years before Josiah's, we find a Godly king who evidently was acquainted with God's Word. Hezekiah "did that which was right in the sight of the Lord (II Kings 18:3; II Chronicles 29:2)." Given the details of Hezekiah's obedience to God in cleansing the land of idolatry, etc., the reader would be foolish to assume that the Godly king just "happened" to do right, without any Scripture to guide him. In fact, his contemporary counterpart in Israel, Hoshea, was taken captive in 722 BC by the Assyrians because, from God's standpoint,

> ... They obeyed not the voice of the Lord their God, but transgressed his covenant, and all that Moses the servant of the Lord commanded, and would not hear them, nor do them (II Kings 18:12).

Thus, six years into Hezekiah's reign, the Northern Kingdom was judged for willfully rejecting God's written

Word. This is not just the opinion of a later writer about why Israel was taken captive--it is the inspired record of God which tells us this. The willful rejection of the writings of Moses clearly implies that such writings were accessible, if Hoshea and Israel had desired to obey them. This seems to be reinforced by the stated fact of Hezekiah's contrasting obedience.

Manasseh, Hezekiah's successor, became king in Judah approximately fifty-seven years before Josiah did. Manasseh rejected God's Word, as is seen in the notations of II Kings 21:7-8 and II Chronicles 33:7-8, both of which reveal that Manasseh specifically violated the Word of God as given to David, Solomon, and Moses. Such a specific indictment seems to indicate that Manasseh also acted willfully, in violation of a written Word to which he had access.

Since Amon, Manasseh's successor, only lasted two years on the throne (II Chronicles 33:20-21), Judah had not gone more than a generation without God's Word until it was found in the Temple in the eighteenth year of Josiah (II Chronicles 34:8-14). Therefore, this story does not *deny*, but rather *confirms,* the promise of Isaiah (who was contemporary with Hezekiah), that God's Word would be accessible to every generation (Isaiah 59:21).

New Testament history records the preservation of the Old Testament, despite the fact that original manuscripts were by then non-existent. Abraham said to the rich man, "They have Moses and the prophets (Luke 16:29). . . ." Abraham did not say that the rich man's brothers had "relatively accurate copies of Moses and the prophets," nor is there any justification for reading this into the statement. Without having the *autographa*, they had the *words* of the *autographa*. In like manner, Jesus told His contemporaries, "Search the scriptures (John 5:39). . . ." These statements seem to imply that the Word of God was readily available to individuals in New Testament times. Despite the fact that they did not have the original writing *materials*, which had long since deteriorated, the important issue was that they still had the original *words*, by God's preservation.

In one of the classic passages about verbal inspiration (II Timothy 3:16) there is evidence of preservation, for Timothy knew the Scriptures from his early childhood (v 15). Fair hermeneutics would demand that the verbally-inspired Scriptures of v 16 were identical in content with those Scriptures which Timothy knew in v 15, despite the fact that different Greek words for "Scripture" were used in the two verses. This seems verified by the fact that the Scriptures Timothy knew in v 15 were called "holy." The word "holy" would not apply to writings that were flawed. Thus, even though Timothy did not have any original Hebrew MSS, some of which had been written at least fifteen centuries earlier, he still had accurately-preserved copies that were precise duplications of that which had been "God-breathed."

In a similar fashion, Peter knew that he had a "more sure word of prophecy," which was the same thing that "holy men of God spake as they were moved by the Holy Ghost (II Peter 1:19, 21)." Actually, there are many statements in the Bible that give promises of, or evidence for, the preservation of God's Word. Some examples are Psalm 33:11; 100:5; 111:7-8; 117:2; 119:89-90, 144, 160; Isaiah 40:8; Matthew

5:18; 24:35; Luke 21:33; John 10:35; Acts 7:38; and I Peter 1:25. Many more could be added to this list.

One passage that is used by many to support the preservation and resultant accessibility of the Word of God is Psalm 12:6-7:

> The words of the LORD *are* pure words: *as* silver tried in a furnace of earth, purified seven times. Thou shalt keep them, O LORD, thou shalt preserve them from this generation for ever.

In the first printing of a previous book,[74] this author drew a conclusion about the passage above that needs to be corrected. While there is, in the Hebrew text, a gender discordance between "words" (feminine) in verse six and the pronoun "them" (masculine) in verse seven, it is not proper to say that it is grammatically *impossible* for the two to be referring to the same thing. In fact, Thomas Strouse gives examples of the same type of gender discordance used elsewhere in the Psalms in connection with God's Word (Psalm 119:11, 129, 152).[75] Thus, it is certainly possible to use this passage to support the doctrine of the preservation of God's Word, although the gender discordance and the tenor of the surrounding context may allow those who disagree with the preservation concept to debate it in the passage under consideration. Because of this controversial grammatical issue, Psalm 12:6-7 may not be the best passage to use when debating with those who deny that the preservation of Scripture is taught in the Bible. Regardless of this issue, the doctrine of the preservation of the Scripture is clearly taught in many other places, such as the passages cited earlier.

At least one textual critic who opposes the TR position on the text realizes that it is a consistent position to hold, if Bible preservation is a doctrine taught in the Scriptures. A noted Greek grammarian and textual critic, Daniel Wallace, has written an attempt to refute the Majority Text (MT) position, of which the TR is a stream. His premise is that the Majority Text advocates hold their position on the basis of a belief that the Bible teaches its own preservation, which view Wallace rejects. Of this concept he says:

> Many MT defenders argue for preservation just as strongly as do TR advocates without noticing that to grant to preservation the same doctrinal status as verbal inspiration is to deny their own claims for the MT and to affirm the TR.[76]

Wallace further states, "TR advocates . . . are the only ones who can claim any kind of consistency in this regard. . . ."[77] Wallace's disdain for the TR position is seen in his statement that, ". . . a wholesale defense of the TR is stripped naked at the bar of logic and empiricism."[78] In Wallace's view, then, the doctrinal beliefs of TR advocates disagree with "logic and empiricism." This leads him to state:

> In sum, a theological *a priori* has no place in textual criticism. Since this is the case, it is necessary to lay aside fideism in dealing with the evidence. . . . With the faith stance of the traditionalists in place, textual criticism becomes so intertwined with orthodoxy that the evidence cannot be objectively interpreted.[79]

Since "fideism" is another word for "faith," Wallace is saying that faith must be laid aside, in order to "objectively" interpret the empirical "evidence" that seems to favor the minority of manuscripts upon which his position is based. Followers of this view should take note of Hebrews 11:6, and realize that one cannot please God by laying aside faith. Wallace decries *theological* dogmatism regarding preservation of Scripture,[80] but is very dogmatic *historically* about the text, making assertions about a text he claims *did not exist* in the first four centuries AD,[81] based upon an argument from silence (no TR-type manuscript has yet been found). As for this view, the Apostle Paul sheds some light with the statement, "God forbid: yea, let God be true, but every man a liar (Romans 3:4). . . ."

A Bible-believer might have difficulty explaining to a scientist, on the bases of reason and empirical evidence, how the sun and moon stood still in Joshua's day (Joshua 10:12-14). Although there are questions the scientist may raise that would be difficult to answer on his accepted bases for authority, the fact of the miracle is not negated by that difficulty. One can still, by faith, consider it a fact, and do so on much surer ground (the Word of God) than that upon which the scientist relies (reason and empiricism).

Wallace is not alone among CT advocates in heavy reliance upon logic and empiricism to defend his position. One author states that, ". . . the most popular method of textual study is the rational, a term indicating that the problem is reasoned out."[82] These same criteria are emphasized by faculty members of Central Baptist Theological Seminary,[83] while denying that the Scriptures teach their own preservation. This denial takes the form of establishing their own five-fold criteria for determining whether the Scriptures teach this principle or not, including stipulations that they already know are contrary to fact:

> "The specific issue is whether any of those passages constitutes a promise that God will preserve the actual *words* of the original documents of Scripture; that He will preserve *all* of those words and *only* those words; that He will preserve them in a particular manuscript, text, or translation; and that He will do so in a publicly accessible way (*emphasis theirs*). The authors of this book propose that any promise that is less specific than this is insufficient as a scriptural basis for the appeal to faith. We recognize that the King James-Only advocates need to find only a single passage of Scripture that makes this promise.[84]

By demanding that *only* those words be preserved, the "well" of logic and Biblical research is "poisoned," since it is clearly obvious that *other* words do, in fact, exist. The concepts that God promised to preserve *all* of the words and make them *accessible are* demonstrated in Scripture (Proverbs 22:20-21; Isaiah 59:21; Matthew 5:18), but the CT position does not accept those two ideas. To arbitrarily add further restrictions before the position can be considered Biblical is to function in the same way that Westcott and Hort did, in subjectively positing their own criteria for textual criticism. It does not seem to be a defensible position that causes one to deny two things that God clearly said, just because the critic has added other criteria into the mix.

Why would it not be more plausible to demand that CT proponents provide Biblical evidence that the words of Scripture would be *not accessible* for fourteen centuries, as their system demands? What Scripture can be used to prove that *a single one* of God's words would be lost? What evidence can be found in God's Word to indicate that local churches for centuries would base their doctrinal statements upon a "spurious" I John 5:7, or that they would be "deluded" into teaching the story of the woman taken in adultery in John 8? What passage of Scripture can be cited to convince us to expect that we would now have merely a "relatively accurate" Bible? Without these proofs given in the Bible, why should anyone accept the Critical Text position?

Harding makes an attempt to justify his CT position from Scripture in this way: "God has promised to preserve His Word through secondary causation (Ps. 119:152), but not through a *miraculous transmission* (*emphasis his*) of the text." [85]

It must be noted, however, that Psalm 119:152 says nothing about "secondary causation." Harding considers only two possibilities: (1) secondary causation, which is subject to error; and (2) miraculous transmission, which is the same as initial inspiration. But it is still faulty reasoning, for even if God had used Harding's term of "secondary causation" in Psalm 119:152, would that mean that He would not have preserved it accurately? Why would *any* method of preservation that God chose to use be subject to error, if God is the one doing the preserving? If God has promised to *preserve* His Word, then it has been *preserved*! Not only does Harding's view add an unwarranted concept to this passage of Scripture, but it also does not account for the previously-noted Scriptures which promise that man could know the "certainty of the words of truth" through preservation. Thus, Harding is both "adding to" and "taking away from" God's Word. Followers of this view should take note of Deuteronomy 4:2 and Revelation 22:18-19.

Further, if God's Word has *not* been preserved, one wonders when it was lost. People who were contemporaries of Moses, Isaiah, Paul, etc., had access to the *autographa*, or the original manuscripts. How long did it take for those manuscripts to disintegrate? At what point did believers realize that their Bibles were deficient? Did those Bibles become worse and worse over the centuries until Westcott and Hort "upgraded" them? A perusal of doctrinal statements by Christians over the centuries of local church history does not reveal any awareness that the Scriptures were lost. Were they all deluded? Those who deny the preservation of God's Word have some serious historical questions to answer, but they also have even more serious *theological* questions to answer.

The TR view acknowledges that God has kept His promise to make His Word accessible to every generation after its writing, despite the fact that archaeologists have not found indisputable TR-type manuscripts from the first four centuries. Should not Bible-believers place more confidence in the Word of God than they do in the suppositions of archaeologists? At one time, those who followed the archaeologists denied the existence and/or Biblical record of the Hittites, Jericho, Ai, etc., but further discoveries simply confirmed the Bible's statements in these cases and many others. God's promise to preserve His Word and make it accessible for every generation leads one to believe that the same local church usage of the TR-type texts that is historically-demonstrated from the fifth century until now, must have been true during the earliest historical period, from which there remains so little information. The primary value of Daniel Wallace's work in this area is to see that those who *do* see preservation as a Bible doctrine are most consistent when they take the TR position on the text. This author is in total agreement with Wallace in that regard!

What have we learned in this chapter?

1. God promised to preserve His Word for each generation.

2. If preservation is a doctrine, the TR position is the most consistent.

Chapter 5

Accomplishment

The fourth Biblical principle of textual criticism is that of accomplishment. God said:

> So shall my word be that goeth forth out of my mouth: it shall not return unto me void, but it shall accomplish that which I please, and it shall prosper *in the thing* whereto I sent it (Isaiah 55:11).

By way of application, students who desire to know which texts best represent God's Word should look to those that have been used by God to impact souls for Him over an extended period of time, rather than to those which have been "shelved" for many centuries and not put to use.

While some may again use the worn-out argument that the latter part of Isaiah has eschatological implications, this does not nullify its application to the rest of Scripture. The context of this chapter clearly presents Bible truths that are not affected by Dispensational changes. Surely, the promise of pardon to the repentant that is seen in verse seven of this chapter has application today, as does the notation in verses eight and nine that God's thoughts and ways are superior to man's. Since God is immutable, and His attributes are consistent, it stands to reason that what He says about His Word transcends the Dispensations. It is mystifying that some who consider themselves Bible-believers think that God's Word about future prophecy will be preserved and effective, while not making that same application to the rest of His Word.

"Word," in Isaiah 55:11, is the same Hebrew term used in Isaiah 59:21, except that it is singular here. "Return" is שוב, a word most commonly translated "turn," "return," or "repent," used 1,066 times in the Old Testament. It has the concept of a change of direction. Since it appears here in the Imperfect tense, it refers to incompleted action, or an ongoing condition. In this case, stated with the negative, it will *not ever come back* to God without accomplishing its intended purpose.

"Void" (ריקם) could be translated "empty," "vain," or "worthless (TWOT)." This word is used to describe a pit with no water (Genesis 37:24), and unfulfilled desires (Isaiah 29:8). It seems, then, to speak of that which is useless, and God says that such will *not ever* be the case with His Word.

Both "shall accomplish" and "shall prosper" are Perfect-tense verbs, which tense normally denotes completed action. The Hebrew language often employs the Perfect tense in prophecy, to indicate a future state or event that is so certain to happen that it is already considered to be completed. Therefore, the accomplishment and prosperity indicated are absolutely certain.

"Accomplish" (עשה) is a word most often translated, "do," or "make," appearing 2,633 times in the Old Testament. The notation of TWOT is useful here:

> When used of God, the word frequently emphasizes God's acts in the sphere of history. These contexts stress one of the most basic concepts of OT theology, i.e., that God is not only transcendent, but he is also immanent in history, effecting his sovereign purpose.[86]

The idea of God's immanence indicates his indwelling, or involvement in human affairs. It seems, then, that the sovereign God will see to it that His Word is effective. Prosper" means "to accomplish satisfactorily what is intended (TWOT)." Used with a negative, it describes the worthlessness of a rotten cloth, in Jeremiah 13:7.

God's Word, when it saturates a man's thinking, also helps that man to accomplish what God desires. This is noted in the challenge recorded in Joshua 1:8:

> This book of the law shall not depart out of thy mouth; but thou shalt meditate therein day and night, that thou mayest observe to do according to all that is written therein: for then thou shalt make thy way prosperous, and then thou shalt have good success.

Once again, the Word of God is to be in man's "mouth," and it is to saturate his thoughts. This continual meditation will result in obedience to God and success in life. Both "prosperous" and "success" are Hiphil stem Imperfect verbs in the Hebrew, indicating a causative relationship that has continuing effects. Therefore, it is the Word of God in man's "mouth" and thoughts that produces continual accomplishment in his life. Furthermore, the challenge to obey "all that is written therein" implies accessibility to *all* of God's written Word.

In Romans 15:4, the believer is given the following reminder about the Word of God: "For whatsoever things were written aforetime were written for our learning, that we through patience and comfort of the scriptures might have hope." Since verse three is a quotation from Psalm 69:9, the term "whatsoever" (οσος) is an all-inclusive word that refers in its context to the entirety of the Old Testament Scriptures. *All* of the Scriptures are intended to be a source of patience, comfort, and hope for the believer. If everything that qualifies to be called "Scriptures" is intended to accomplish this, it would seem that these benefits would be diminished to whatever degree *any* of it were lost.

A similar concept can be seen from I Corinthians 10:11, where the Scriptures ". . . are written for our admonition. . . ." Thus, they provide our "instruction" and "warning,"(BAG). God's Word further accomplishes man's salvation (John 20:31; II Timothy 3:15), assurance (I John 5:13), conviction (Hebrews 4:12), maturity (II Timothy 3:16-17), and ministry (Acts 18:28). Such significant accomplishments are not based upon "ambiguity" and "conjecture," but upon the "certainty of the words."

When figures of speech used in the Bible to describe itself are noted, the concept of its own accomplishment is emphatically seen. The Word of God is a hammer that breaks the rock in pieces (Jeremiah 23:29), a fire that burns (Jeremiah 5:14), a sword that cuts (Hebrews 4:12), a lamp that enlightens (Psalm 119:105; Proverbs 6:23), water that cleanses (Ephesians 5:26), milk that nourishes (I Peter 2:2), meat that helps believers to mature (Hebrews 5:12-14), and seed that grows (Mark 4:14-15). These accomplishments are not done through uncertainty and conjecture, but through the firm certainty that believers have historically placed in the Bible that was in their hands.

God's Word was not intended to lie unused in a monastery or a library, collecting dust, as seems to have been the case with *Sinaiticus* and *Vaticanus*. These two main sources used by Westcott and Hort in the development of their Critical Text were apparently unused for about fourteen centuries or more of history.

By contrast, history records the extensive usage of the "Byzantine" texts, out of which came the *Textus Receptus* ("Received Text," denoting commonality of use). It is also indisputable that the primary English translation of the TR, the Authorized King James Version, has been greatly used of God over the centuries since its production.

God has used the KJV for four centuries of local church history, notably in the great revival and missionary movements that have impacted multitudes of souls for Christ. Such a powerful "sword" should not be casually laid aside. While some say today that the old KJV is too hard to read, it was not too hard for the common people in Appalachia and all across America to understand, when thousands of local churches were being planted in the eighteenth and nineteenth centuries. This was despite the fact that many of those people were lacking in formal education. None of the modern-day translations and versions of the Bible can claim the impact upon the souls of men that the KJV has produced. It seems clear that the words which God promised to preserve and the local churches have endorsed, have been translated into the English Bible that the Holy Spirit has used to "accomplish" His intended purpose.

God said of His Word that it would be known by its **accuracy, authentication, accessibility, and accomplishment**. Biblical evidence has been given as proof of these criteria, rather than leaving the student with a subjective, unsubstantiated set of "rules" for textual criticism. There may be questions of history that are difficult to answer (owing to the incompleteness of our knowledge of history), but those questions do not pose as big a problem for TR advocates as do the questions that the Scriptures raise against the Critical Text position. With Scripture as a foundation, history can be seen as demonstrating that what God promised about His Word has come to pass, and that the *Textus Receptus* is that which He has preserved through the instrumentality of local churches. The King James Version, as the best English translation of the TR, should not be abandoned, nor replaced by inferior versions which sacrifice accuracy for readability.

What have we learned in this chapter?

1. God promised that His Word would accomplish His purposes.

2. The Critical Text was virtually unused for fourteen centuries.

3. The TR-type texts have been used extensively for centuries.

Chapter 6

W-H Principles of Textual Criticism

A stark contrast will be seen when the Biblical principles of textual criticism are compared to the self-determined principles followed by Westcott and Hort in the collation and evaluation of their Greek manuscripts. Although modern textual critics have altered Westcott and Hort's work, they have not repudiated the principles followed in determining the foundation of this textual position.

One contemporary follower of the CT says it this way:

> The two key figures in the development of the history of the text remain those of Brooke Foss Westcott and Fenton John Anthony Hort. They are of outstanding importance because with them the critical text became reality and the principles of criticism were set forth so clearly and effectively that their influence is still paramount in the field of textual study. As we shall see, some of their ideas have been modified by later scholars, but no new theory of criticism has been developed to replace the one they set forth.[87]

Erwin Nestle, describing the work of his father, Eberhard Nestle, speaks confidently of the process Eberhard followed:

> "He therefore deliberately refrained from . . . subjective, critical examination of the different versions, but took as basis the great scientific editions

of the 19th century of Tischendorf (of Leipzig) and Westcott and Hort.[88]

Another modern critic, George Eldon Ladd, says, "Through the developed science of textual criticism we have achieved a relatively accurate text of the New Testament."[89] While Bible-believers are not satisfied with a "relatively accurate" New Testament, Ladd explains that:

> An evangelical criticism as well as a rationalistic criticism must often be satisfied with hypotheses, probabilities, possibilities, rather than in dogmatic certainties, as distasteful as this may be to the uncritical mind which insists on "thus saith the Lord" in every detail of Bible study.[90]

It would seem from these quotations that Christians who believe God has preserved His Word for every generation, and that the Bible, then, is "sure" and "certain" would be considered as "unscientific" and "uncritical" by the proponents of the Critical Text and its derivatives. In fact, the CT advocates seem to boast that their approach is scientific, with an "elitist" scorn for those who disagree. Already cited is Daniel Wallace's desire for "logic and empiricism" (man's five physical senses) above faith, which he scorns as "fideism."[91]

This prejudice against the Byzantine (TR-type) texts is seen in the following quote from a CT advocate, regarding Codex Alexandrinus, a fifth-century manuscript:

> In the Gospels, it is the oldest representative of the Byzantine text, and thus is not considered very important by many. However, in the remainder of

the New Testament, it represents the Alexandrian text and is one of the most valuable manuscripts.[92]

In other words, the part of Alexandrinus which appears Byzantine is of no value, but the part (of the same manuscript) that supports the CT has great value! Such an absurd statement unmasks the prejudicial spirit among the "scientific" academic community. This prejudice is further seen in the following assessment of the thinking of Westcott and Hort:

> The vast majority of the manuscripts were eliminated as being of little value in the development of the text. Hort was convinced that virtually all of the later uncial manuscripts and almost all the miniscules represented a text of the New Testament that could not be traced back earlier than the fourth century. This textual type was labeled Syrian. . . . Hort was convinced that when only the Syrian text supported a reading, this reading could not be correct. . . . We must remember that it was this Syrian text which lay behind the Received Text. . . .[93]

Westcott and Hort followed nine concepts in evaluating Greek manuscripts, to determine their usefulness for textual criticism. Although they are expressed in complicated terminology, an attempt will be made here to simplify their statements. This runs the risk of *over-simplification*, but at least it can give the reader an approximation of the W-H approach.

Here, then, is a shortened summary of the W-H principles.[94] The first rule is that older readings are to be preferred ("oldest is best"). Second, readings are evaluated on the basis of supposed quality, not quantity. Third, a reading that appears to combine two simpler readings found in differing texts ("conflation") is rejected as being later. Fourth, the reading that makes the best sense is preferred. Fifth, the reading that seems to fit the human author's usual style is chosen. Sixth, The reading that best explains the existence of other readings is selected. Seventh, the reading that appears to be a scribal improvement is rejected. Eighth, harder readings are preferred over smoother ones. And finally, readings are preferred that appear in manuscripts that are already trusted.

Perhaps it would be appropriate to consider these nine principles one at a time, to see how this "scientific" approach fits with what the Bible has said about itself. Concerning the "oldest is best" concept, it seems logical enough on the surface, but there are some distinct problems with this concept. To begin with, has this always been true, that the oldest known manuscripts are the best? If so, for many centuries, the oldest known manuscripts supported the tradition that produced the TR. Was that stream of texts best for fourteen centuries, and then demoted to "second-best" by Westcott and Hort? Did Christians and local churches for centuries follow an inferior Bible? Also, how do the scholars know that the ancient Greek texts which Jerome considered to be older than the fourth-century manuscripts will not be discovered? Would this not then show that the first part of John 8 and the last part of Mark 16 should be included in the New Testament? Would the critics then still insist that "oldest is best?"

In actuality, it has not been demonstrated that *Vaticanus* and *Sinaiticus*, the two main building blocks of the Critical Text position, are the oldest manuscripts.

Westcott and Hort themselves offer the following information:

> A text virtually identical with the prevalent Greek text of the Middle Ages was used by Chrysostom and other Antiochian Fathers in the latter part of the fourth century, and thus must have been represented by MSS as old as any MS now surviving.[95]

That "prevalent Greek text of the Middle Ages" was, of course, the tradition that produced the TR. Regarding the Peshitta, which included passages omitted from the CT, Westcott and Hort say, "External evidence as to its date and history is entirely wanting: but there is no reason to doubt that it is at least as old as the Latin Version."[96] Since Jerome's Latin version was contemporaneous with *Sinaiticus* and Vaticanus, and since he claimed to not use the "recent" (fourth century) manuscripts, these statements by the authors of the CT position leave room to question whether their foundational documents are, in fact, "oldest." They may be the oldest *that have been found*, but they are not necessarily the oldest for which we have evidence of existence.

As for the second concept followed by Westcott and Hort (readings are evaluated on the basis of quality, not quantity), one might suggest that this is a totally subjective way of evaluating the manuscript evidence. It immediately discounts the large number of manuscripts which, by definition, are called the "majority." This supposed "quality" is ascribed to about four hundred manuscripts, in opposition to the approximately five thousand, two hundred and fifty manuscripts that make up the majority. Who is authorized to determine what is "quality" in a Bible manuscript? How is this "quality" determined? Who makes the rules? Why should the reader accept the suggestion that the smaller number of manuscripts are of better "quality" than are the vast majority? Is the "quality" of a manuscript more important than its accuracy and accessibility? Does this all not sound highly subjective? Such subjectivity leads to uncertainty, which the W-H editors freely admit in the following collage of statements that all appear in the same paragraph in Westcott and Hort's explanatory notes:

> ... Reexamination brings to light an ambiguity.... No definite rule can be given... the apparent conflict remains.... The ultimate determination must evidently be here left to personal judgement.... It is manifestly right to abstain from placing before the reader an appearance of greater certainty than really exists... the places where an absolute decision would at present be arbitrary....[97]

The third principle followed in the W-H system uses the term "conflation" to describe a reading that combines the readings in two other manuscripts, and the critical conclusion is that the longer reading is automatically wrong. An example of this is seen in Luke 24:53, where the Alexandrian (Critical-type) text is translated "blessing God," the Western (also Critical-type) text says "praising God," and the Byzantine (TR-type) text says "praising and blessing God." In such a case, the longer reading is supposed by W-H to be a "conflation" of the other two and is automatically disqualified from consideration. Their statement is that, "... erroneous insertion of matter is always antecedently more probable than its erroneous omission...."[98] Why is this? Could it not be that the two smaller versions reflect omissions by their copyists, and that the original language included both terms in the description of the disciples' actions? This rule presupposes that a copyist is more likely to *add* words to the copied text than he is to *omit* them. Is this true? This author's experience points to just the opposite conclusion. If a copyist were to *add* something that did not appear in the original, the copyist would surely be aware of that. On the other hand, an unintentional omission seems much more likely to happen. Why should the student of the Bible accept this third W-H supposition, when the end result is opposition to the vast majority of extant (existing) manuscripts, still leaving questions about which of the two shorter versions is the accurate one?

Principle number four followed by W-H is that preference is given to the reading that makes the most sense. This appears to be a logical approach, in keeping with a high view of the Word of God. Of course, what "makes sense" to one who is enamored with science, logic, and empiricism may not make sense to one who is committed to the verbal preservation of God's Word, as an item of faith. The "sense" that a manuscript seems to present is based upon the textual critic's presuppositions about what the reading should be. Consequently, the same subjectivism that plagues the previously-mentioned principles of textual criticism still exists here.

Rule number five gives preference to the reading that seems to fit the human author's usual style of writing. This also seems reasonable, but the same kind of thinking produced the liberal JEDP theory for the authorship of the Pentateuch, assuming that Moses could not have used two different names for God. Did not the Apostle John use a different writing style in the Revelation from that which he used in his Gospel, and did not these books both differ somewhat in style from his Epistles? It would be hard to imagine that this concept could be incontrovertibly used to solve very many manuscript discrepancies. Once again, the suspicion of subjectivism raises its ugly head.

Westcott and Hort creatively decided that the reading which best explains the existence of other readings is preferred. This sixth rule may be the most subjective of all, to say nothing about its lack of clarity in application. It could well evolve into a "circular reasoning" scenario, where a given reading is accepted because of its compatibility with another reading, which is accepted because of its compatibility with the first. These manuscripts, then, become "self-authenticating," based upon the "rules" established by those who claim to be experts in the field. By what authority are these claims made?

Principle number seven rejects any reading that appears to be a scribal improvement. Once again it must be asked, upon what basis is this judgment made, and what are the authoritative criteria upon which one decides that a reading is a "scribal improvement," rather than being original? Such reasoning led W-H to refer to ". . . the numerous Western readings which owe a deceptive amplitude of apparent authority to the accident that they found favour with the Syrian revisers. . . ."[99]

How could an unprejudiced mind make this choice? Treating the Bible as if it were just like any other ancient historical book is both unsatisfactory and offensive to those who cherish it as the inspired and preserved Word of God.

The eighth principle followed in the W-H method is that harder readings are preferred over the smoother ones. This assumes that God is not a good Communicator, which is another way of saying that the One who created language is unable to use it very well. Not only does this insult God, but it even contradicts two of the other principles used by W-H. The second rule shows preference for "quality" in a manuscript, and the fourth favors that which makes the best sense. This eighth rule seems to say just the opposite. It would appear that the critics wanted to leave a "loophole," so that they could still accept a reading that breaks their other rules, based primarily upon their own prejudices toward it. It is obvious that not *all* of these rules can be followed consistently.

Number nine in the list informs the student that readings are preferred when found in manuscripts that are already trusted. The skeptic might ask, are the manuscripts trusted because of their readings, or are the readings trusted because of the manuscripts in which they appear? Is this materially different from the evolutionary thinking that dates rock strata by the fossils found in them, and then dates the fossils by the kind of rock strata in which they appear? Again, a subjective system that depends upon circular reasoning is uncovered in the W-H method.

To the Bible-believer who acknowledges that the preservation of Scripture is a doctrine taught in the Word of God, there seem to be numerous problems with the procedures followed by self-appointed critics of the Bible. There is no good reason to accept these principles as authoritative, when in practice they treat the Bible as any other ancient document and do not even take into account what the Bible has said about itself. This attitude is reflected in the following statement:

The undisputed reign of the Received Text began to break down in 1831 with the work of Carl Lachmann (1793-1851). Perhaps the fact that he was not a theologian assisted him in making the break with the Received Text. He was a professor of classical philology in Berlin. As such, he had studied the texts of many of the ancient Greek writers and had published of their writings. He believed that the same principles could be used to establish the text of the New Testament.[100]

It seems, then, that this advocate of the CT position feels that Biblical study would be a deterrent to his view. It is quite clear that this "scientific" approach, which treats the Bible as if it were any other ancient document, does not attempt to take into account what the Bible has to say about itself. Perhaps theological knowledge might make that "break" from the TR more difficult to make!

No matter what textual position one takes, there are some historical difficulties. Critics have attacked the work of Erasmus, particularly with regard to the last few verses of the Book of the Revelation. However, the two main manuscripts upon which the CT is dependent are clearly suspect when it comes to the Revelation. *Sinaiticus* (א) and *Vaticanus* (**B**) have been acknowledged by Westcott and Hort to be deficient in what they call the "Apocalypse:"

> Whether **B** ever contained the Apocalypse or not, it is now defective from Hebrews ix 14 onward. The loss is the greater because in the Apocalypse א has a text conspicuously inferior to its text of the other books, partly inherited from earlier more or less corrupted texts. . . .[101]

The incompleteness of present-day knowledge about the events of the earliest centuries of local church history leaves the critics in a mode of guesswork about what manuscripts were actually available to those saints. However, those who follow the CT position not only have *historical* questions they cannot answer, but they also have *theological* issues that they have not properly addressed, particularly in their attempt to downplay the numerous passages of Scripture which teach the preservation and accessibility of God's Word for every generation of mankind.

Therefore, rather than feeling intimidated by the prevailing "scholarship," which denies that the Scripture teaches its own preservation, the student of the Word of God must *start with faith* in that teaching, and give credence to the textual tradition which allows for such preservation. Consistently followed, this belief will place one squarely in the TR camp. Within that tradition, the consideration of translations then becomes relevant.

What have we learned in this chapter?

1. The Critical Text method claims to be "scientific."

2. The Critical Text principles are highly subjective, not truly scientific.

3. It is better to have unanswered questions in *history* than in *theology*.

Chapter 7

What about the New King James Version?

Those who acknowledge the authority of the *Textus Receptus* face another issue: that is, which English translation is to be preferred? Both the old King James and the New King James claim to be translated from the TR, so a decision must be made between these two versions. The Biblical requirements of authenticity and accomplishment seem to favor the old King James Version over the New King James, because of its long history of use (four hundred years). But what about the matter of accuracy?

In approaching this subject, it should be noted that there is no theological reason (no statement from God) to believe that a *translation* into any language would be inspired in the same way that the original writings in Hebrew and Greek were. No translation has been "God-breathed," as II Timothy 3:16 says of the originals. However, the same thing could be said of copies, yet the New Testament consistently speaks as if first-century Christians had access to the very words of the originals. Copies of Scripture reflect "inspiration" to the degree that they accurately represent the originals, and in a similar fashion, translations reflect a "derived inspiration" to the degree that they accurately translate those accurate copies. Therefore, *accuracy* in a translation becomes more important than *readability*.

Some have attacked the work of Erasmus in developing the Greek New Testament upon which the KJV is based. Donald L. Brake suggests that Basel printer Johann Froben, motivated by "the economic advantages of being the first to publish," enlisted Erasmus to quickly produce a Greek New Testament.[102] Brake adds, "The pressure of a short deadline forced Erasmus to produce an imperfect and inferior edition."[103]

However, these statements refer to the first edition of Erasmus, which was published in 1516. Brake later says:

> The King James translators used the 1588-89 or 1598 Beza New Testaments, which were essentially the same as Erasmus' third edition (1522), the 1550 Stephanus, the 1565 Beza, and the 1633 Elzevir editions.[104]

Thus, it was not the 1516 edition of Erasmus' work that became the standardized text of the Greek New Testament and the basis of the King James Version. This means that the criticisms of the few manuscripts that Erasmus originally used and his haste in preparation are not fair assessments of the facts, when they are cited in relation to the KJV.

Erasmus' 1516 edition omitted the statement which supports the Trinity in I John 5:7.[105] Lopez de Stunica challenged Erasmus to correct this, and presented a Greek manuscript (Codex Montfortianus) that included the passage, so Erasmus added it to his 1522 edition.[106] Brake personally examined Codex Montfortianus, to see if it had been tampered with or revised by Stunica, to falsely "document" the reading for I John 5:7, but Brake's conclusion was that the manuscript showed no evidence of having been altered.[107] Since Brake is not a TR advocate, his honesty is especially appreciated in this matter.

Whereas the KJV was produced in 1611 and revised to accommodate changes in the English language in 1769, the NKJV was produced in three stages, with the complete Bible published in 1982. Explanations of the NKJV's translation philosophy and procedures, plus a list of endorsers of the new version are given by its editor, Arthur L. Farstad, in a book published in 1989.[108] Farstad notes, ". . . This little volume is intended to show we didn't just 'change the *thees* and *thous*'!"[109]

The endorsers of the NKJV include, among others, leaders from AWANA, Child Evangelism Fellowship, Campus Crusade, Word of Life, the Evangelical Church, Pentecostal Church, Presbyterian Church, Bible Church, Southern Baptist Convention, National Baptist Convention, Liberty University, Wycliffe College, BIOLA, Concordia Seminary, and Theological Seminary of the Reformed Episcopal Church.[110]

The listing is totally devoid of Independent Baptist leaders. One wonders whether the NKJV committee could not find any such endorsers, or if they perhaps did not want any. In fairness, it should be noted that the editor of the Old Testament for the NKJV, Dr. James Price, is an Independent Baptist, but the question still remains concerning endorsements by leaders of the movement, and Price himself is definitely not a TR advocate. At any rate, it seems as if there was an attempt to appeal to a fairly broad range of theological positions, apparently encouraging those who identify with the listed groups to be comfortable with the new version.

The desire expressed by the NKJV editor is admirable: ". . . The leading concern of those who love

God's Word is that a version of the Scriptures be a translation that is *accurate* (*emphasis his*)."[111] Unfortunately, this goal was not satisfactorily accomplished in the NKJV. Some examples of this failure will be noted.

In Genesis 2:18, where the KJV speaks of the woman as an "help meet" for her husband, the NKJV calls her a "helper comparable" to him. The quoted portions show each version's rendering of one Hebrew word, עזר, which means "helper." The KJV emphasizes that this helper is "meet," or sufficient for the man, but the NKJV seems to reveal a desire for "political correctness," attempting to focus on the equality of the man and woman. There is no reason to see this word as indicating "comparable," especially since it is used many times in the Old Testament to refer to God as man's Helper. In each of those cases, it is very clear that God is a "sufficient" Helper to man, and not "comparable" to him. There is certainly no justification from the Hebrew language for this change being made in the NKJV.

Genesis 22:8 has always blessed the hearts of KJV readers as Abraham tells Isaac, ". . . God will provide himself a lamb . . . ." The Hebrew language gives no reason for the NKJV to change to, "God will provide for Himself the lamb . . . ." The KJV leaves open the possibility that God Himself will be the Lamb, and this has great prophetic significance as a Messianic prophecy. When the NKJV adds the word "for," it diminishes that dual application concept.

The NKJV translation of Psalm 109:6 changes the name "Satan" to "an accuser." The KJV "Satan" is simply the Hebrew word שטן pronounced and spelled in equivalent English letters (transliteration). Of course, the word means "accuser," but this is not just *any* accuser—this is Satan himself.

Isaiah 66:5 in the KJV uses the phrase, "he shall appear," but the NKJV changes this to "we may see." Since the Hebrew verb is in a third person, singular form, the KJV is correct and the NKJV in error.

Random samplings of differences in the two versions can also be seen in the New Testament. One of the most serious errors in the NKJV is seen in Matthew 21:32, where the KJV "ye . . . repented not" is revised in the NKJV to read, "ye did not . . . relent." The Greek word μεταμελλομαι does not warrant this change.

The "Comforter" in John 14:16 is changed to "Helper" in the NKJV. The "Godhead" in Acts 17:29 becomes "Divine Nature" in the new version. In Acts 24:14, "heresy" is changed to "sect," when the KJV term is simply a transliteration that identifies false teaching. "Require," in I Corinthians 1:22 becomes "request" in the NKJV. "Imaginations," in II Corinthians 10:5 is newly rendered "arguments." The "heretick" of Titus 3:10 has been turned into a "divisive man" in the NKJV. "Heaven" in Revelation 6:14 is changed to "sky" in the new version. Many more such instances could be cited, but these samplings point to the conclusion that the NKJV is not as accurate as the KJV.

This author did a word-for-word comparison of the KJV and the NKJV in the books of Genesis, Romans, and Revelation. The results are detailed in Appendices A, B, and C at the end of this book, but a summary will be given here. Where there were differences, they were evaluated. A change in word order was not considered to be a discrepancy, nor was the substitution of "you" instead of "ye," *etc.* When more significant differences appeared, Hebrew and Greek lexicons were consulted, to see if both translations were allowed. If so, then it was still not considered to be a discrepancy. Of course, the lexicons were written in the more modern style of English, so this approach actually favored the NKJV more than it did the KJV. Since it would be a totally unfair comparison to fail to account for the "antiquated" words in the KJV, elimination of those differences was the final step in the process.

Taking that approach, viewing 40,036 words in the KJV for the book of Genesis, there still were found 408 discrepancies in the NKJV. The KJV was seen to agree more with the Hebrew lexicons in 79% of the discrepancies, and once the antiquated terminology was taken into account, the number swelled to an amazing 88% in favor of the KJV!

Similar steps were taken in Romans and Revelation, consulting Greek lexicons to resolve the differences. In Romans, where the KJV uses 4,325 words, 163 discrepancies were found, and the final conclusion was that the KJV was more true to the Greek language in 63% of the differences. A comparison of the 6,165 words in the Revelation revealed exactly 100 discrepancies, with the KJV translating the Greek more accurately in 77 of those places.

Many of the observed differences can be explained by the fact that the NKJV translators often told what they felt the passage *meant*, rather than strictly translating what the original languages *said*. It is not that the NKJV should be considered heretical, because it does not teach false doctrines. It could, however, be seen to be considerably less accurate than the KJV. It is supposed to be a *Bible*, not a *commentary*.

> # What have we learned in this chapter?
>
> 1. Translations have a "derived authority," based upon accuracy.
>
> 2. The KJV is superior in accuracy to the NKJV.
>
> 3. Bibles should be chosen on the basis of *accuracy*, rather than *readability*.

Chapter 8

Conclusion

The Bible gives statements about itself that are helpful in the evaluation of Greek and Hebrew manuscripts. Instead of accepting the subjective concepts followed by the proponents of the Critical Text, the Bible-believer should use the God-given criteria for selecting the texts that rightfully constitute the Word of God.

Mere human logic must give way to the faith that gives God credit for keeping His promises to preserve His Word for every generation of mankind. Since God has given indications of the accuracy, authentication, accessibility, and accomplishment of His Word, one can look at history and see which texts meet these Biblical criteria.

The answer is that the *Textus Receptus* position, among all the choices that textual critics face, is the most consistent, as even a prominent critic of that position has stated.[112] The subjectively-contrived, "scientific" Critical Text, which depends upon the "oldest found and least used" Greek texts, should be relegated to the category of ". . . oppositions of science falsely so called (I Timothy 6:20)."

Contrary to modern popular opinion, the Bible must not be treated as if it were merely any other book of antiquity, disregarding its supernatural nature and that of its Author. The God Who promised to preserve His Word and make it accessible to every generation has chosen to use the local churches of this Dispensation to be the vehicles of that preservation, so it is to the local churches of history, rather than to the "scholars" that the Christian must look for his

Bible. Whereas modern-day churches have begun to turn away from the text that has been traditionally accepted, this is a recent phenomenon, rather than a consistent trend in history.

To those who claim to be conservative Bible-believers still clinging to the CT, a challenge is issued. Either they should (1) exegetically deal with the passages of Scripture referred to here and demonstrate that they do *not* say what they clearly appear to say; (2) admit that they place more credence upon logic and empiricism than they do upon the Scripture; or (3) change their position to espouse the TR. Some boast of how many books they have read on the subject of the text of Scripture, but it looks as if their list of books does not include Deuteronomy, Proverbs, Psalms, Isaiah, Matthew, I Timothy, etc.

What Scripture teaches us to anticipate a *loss of Scripture* at any point in history? What Bible verse counteracts the concept seen in Proverbs 22:21 about the "certainty of the words?" Is there a single verse in the Bible that predicts a time when God's Word would either be uncertain or inaccessible? Where in the Bible does the God Who expects man to live ". . . by every word that proceedeth out of the mouth of God," tell us that we will not *have* every word? These questions must be answered before credence is given to the subjective interpretations of historical data, about which even the "experts," with their "scientific" approach are not unanimous. It seems that, not only is the CT position based upon an argument from *historical silence* (that early TR-type manuscripts have not yet been found), but even more significantly, it is based upon an argument from *Biblical silence* (drawing conclusions about the Scripture that are not found in Scripture). Worse still, they deny, or at best ignore, the many passages of the Bible which teach its own preservation, accessibility, and certainty.

Once the Bible-believer has settled upon the *Textus Receptus* for his New Testament in Greek, the English translations of that Greek text can be compared for accuracy. Although the marketing ploy of today demands that "readability" and personal preferences should dictate which Bible to purchase, it is not God Who has given these criteria. Thus, the believer who desires to please God should choose the translation which best represents the meanings of the Greek words of the *Textus Receptus*. The same could be said for the Hebrew Masoretic Text of the Old Testament.

At this point, the primary debate among TR advocates is between the King James Version and the New King James Version. Some of the reasons to prefer the old KJV above the NKJV have been cited above, and a great deal of documentation from the books of Genesis, Romans, and Revelation will be given in the appendices to follow. The principle difference seems to be that the KJV focuses on what God *said*, while the NKJV attempts to describe what the translators think God *meant*. This is important, for when one pays for a *Bible*, he does not expect to be getting a *commentary*.

The pragmatic reasoning offered by some is that they have children and new converts who, they assume, cannot understand the terminology of the KJV. But most of those same churches have believers who have been saved for many years, who *could* understand the KJV, and the churches still do not recommend the most accurate Bible for those people! It could also be noted that there are local churches still using the KJV, who successfully use it with children and new converts, so it is certainly possible for that to be done. Just as new converts should be educated in theological terminology, such as justification, sanctification, propitiation, etc., they may also need to be educated in the matter of the "antiquated" terminology of the most accurate English version of the Scriptures.

It would seem, then, more consistent to not only prefer the *Textus Receptus* for one's Greek text, but for those who desire an English Bible to choose the old King James Version. Whether one considers one translation more "readable" or not, the Bible-believer should desire accuracy above all other considerations when choosing a translation of God's Word. This allows for the reader of the Bible to experience the "certainty of the words" of the Scripture.

Taking God's Word at face value, then, the student of the Bible can choose the Hebrew Masoretic Text for the Old Testament, the Greek *Textus Receptus* for the New Testament, and the King James Version as the best English translation of those original language texts.

Appendix A

Differences in NKJV/KJV in Genesis

(There are 40,036 words in KJV for Genesis)

In the following analysis, the NKJV rendering in each verse appears first, separated from the KJV by /, and the comment that follows reflects research from Hebrew lexicons (BDB and TWOT). Heb is an abbreviation for the Hebrew language.

1:20 "living" / "moving. . . that hath life" (Heb supports KJV)

1:20 "across the face" / "in the open" (Heb supports NKJV)

1:21 "sea creatures" / "whales" (Heb supports NKJV)

1:29 "yields" / "bearing" (Heb supports KJV)

1:29 "fruit" / "fruit of a tree" (Heb supports KJV)

1:31 "indeed" / "behold" (Heb supports KJV)

2:4 "history" / "generations" (Heb supports KJV)

2:18 "helper comparable" / "help meet" (Heb supports KJV. NKJV seems to use "Political correctness.") Since God is frequently man's "helper," the word does not primarily denote a peer-level comparison, but the appropriateness of the help seems more likely.

2:24 "joined" / "cleave" (Heb supports KJV, because of Qal stem)

3:1 "cunning" / "subtil" (Heb supports KJV)

3:7 "coverings" / "aprons" (Heb supports KJV)

4:2 "this time" is added (Heb supports KJV)

4:7 "it (sin)" / "his (Abel)" (Heb uses masculine suffix, supporting KJV)

5:2 "called them Mankind" / "called their name Adam" (Heb word for "name" is in text, supporting KJV)

6:5 "intent" / "imagination" (Heb supports KJV)

7:2,3 "seven each" / "by sevens" (Heb word for 7 is given twice in succession. The same pattern is found in 7:15, with the number 2, and NKJV translates it "two by two", so this indicates that the KJV is superior)

7:3 "species" / "seed" (Heb supports KJV)

7:4,23 "all living things" / "every living substance" (Heb supports KJV)

7:14 "bird . . . bird" / "fowl . . . bird" (two different Heb words are used, so KJV is accurate)

7:18; 8:13 "surface" / "face" (Heb supports KJV. Same word in 8:8,9, where both translate it "face")

7:22 "breath of the spirit" / "breath" (Heb has 2 words, so Heb supports NKJV)

7:23 "air" / "heaven" (Heb supports KJV)

8:3 "receded" / "returned" (Heb supports KJV)

8:8, 11 "receded" / "abated" (different Heb from 8:3, but Heb supports KJV)

8:12 "waited" / "stayed" (Heb supports NKJV)

8:19 "families" / "kinds" (Heb supports NKJV, and this is normally "family" elsewhere in KJV)

8:21 "destroy" / "smite" (Heb supports KJV)

9:16 "populated" / "overspread" (Heb supports KJV)

9:23 "turned away" / "backward" (Heb supports KJV)

9:27 "may God enlarge" / "God shall enlarge" (Heb uses Hiphil, which is causative, favoring KJV)

10:5 "coastland peoples" / "isles" (Heb supports KJV)

10:11 "(Nimrod) went to Assyria and built Nineveh" / "went forth Asshur and builded Nineveh" (Heb supports KJV, because "to" is not in the Heb text)

10:11 "Rehoboth Ir" / "the city Rehoboth" (Heb supports KJV, since *ir* in Heb means "city", and is translated that way in v 12, in both versions)

10:12 "principle city" / "great city" (Heb supports KJV)

10:16 "the Jebusite" / "and the Jebusite" (Heb uses the conjunction in support of KJV, whereas the omission of it might allow the interpretation that Heth begat the Jebusite, rather than Canaan. In fact, the conjunction is consistently found in the Hebrew, but omitted by NKJV 12 times in vv 13-18)

10:19 "as far as" / "as thou comest to" (Heb supports KJV, and the same Heb usage later in the same verse is translated similarly in both versions)

11:3 "bake" / "burn" (Heb supports KJV)

11:6 "withheld" / "restrained" (Heb supports KJV)

11:6 "purpose" / "imagined" (Heb supports NKJV)

12:5 "people" / "souls" (Heb supports KJV)

12:6 "terebinth tree" / "plain" (Heb supports NKJV. This is true in 4 places in Genesis)

12:6 "Canaanites" / "Canaanite" (Heb supports KJV)

12:7 "descendants" / "seed" (Heb supports KJV)

12:10 "dwell" / "sojourn" (Heb supports KJV)

12:10 "severe" / "grievous" (Heb supports KJV)

12:11 "of beautiful countenance" / "fair to look upon" (Heb supports KJV)

12:13 "I" / "my soul" (Heb supports KJV)

12:19 "here is" / "behold" (Heb supports KJV)

13:3 "journey" / "journeys" (Heb supports KJV)

13:7 "Perizzites" / "Perizzite" (Heb supports KJV)

14:5, 7 "attacked" / "smote" (Heb supports KJV)

14:9 "against" / "with" (Heb supports KJV)

14:10 "mountains" / "mountain" (Heb supports KJV)

14:15 "his forces" / "himself" (Heb supports KJV)

14:15 "north" / "left hand" (NKJV is interpreting, rather than translating. Heb supports KJV)

14:17 "defeat" / "slaughter" (Heb supports KJV)

14:20 "a tithe" / "tithes" (Heb supports NKJV)

15:4 "body" / "bowels" (Heb supports KJV)

15:5 "outside" / "abroad" (Heb supports NKJV)

15:11 "vultures" / "fowls" (Heb supports KJV)

15:12 "horror and great darkness" / "horror of great darkness" (Heb supports KJV)

15:17 "there appeared" is added in NKJV, without Heb support

16:5 "embrace" / "bosom" (Heb supports KJV)

16:6, 8 "presence" / "face" (Heb supports KJV)

16:10 "they shall not" / "it shall not" (Heb supports KJV)

16:15 "named his son" / "called his son's name" (Heb supports KJV)

17:9 "as for you" is added in NKJV, without Heb support

17:11 "ye shall be circumcised" / "ye shall circumcise" (Heb supports KJV)

17:11 "foreskins" / "foreskin" (Heb supports NKJV)

17:16 "peoples" / "people" (Heb supports NKJV)

17:19 "no" is added in NKJV, without Heb support

17:22 "finished" / "left off" (Heb supports NKJV)

17:23 "foreskins" / "foreskin" (Heb supports NKJV)

18:5 "refresh" / "comfort" (Heb supports KJV)

18:11 "passed the age of childbearing" / "ceased . . . after the manner of women" (Heb supports KJV)

18:19 "I have known" / "I know" (Heb supports NKJV)

18:19 "in order that" / "that" (Heb supports KJV)

18:20 "grave" / "grievous" (Heb supports KJV)

18:28 "five less" / "lack five" (Heb supports KJV)

19:2 "here now" / "behold" (Heb supports KJV)

19:2 "way" / "ways" (Heb supports NKJV)

19:2 "open square" / "street" (Heb supports NKJV)

19:3 "insisted" / "pressed" (Heb supports KJV)

19:8 "as you wish" / "good in your eyes" (Heb supports KJV)

19:10 "hands" / "hand" (Heb supports KJV)

19:15 "dawned" / "arose" (Heb supports KJV)

19:16 "hands" / "hand" (Heb supports KJV)

19:18 "lords" / "Lord" (Heb supports KJV)

19:19 "increased" / "magnified" (Heb supports KJV)

19:30 "mountains" / "mountain" (Heb supports KJV)

19:32, 34 "lineage" / "seed" (Heb supports KJV)

19:38 "people" / "children" (Heb supports KJV)

20:1 "south" / "south country" (Heb supports KJV)

20:8 "hearing" / "ears" (Heb supports KJV)

20:10 "have in view" / "saw" (Heb supports KJV)

20:12 "truly" is added in NKJV, without Heb support

20:13 "do" / "shew" (Heb supports NKJV)

20:16 "vindicates" / "covering of the eyes" (Heb supports KJV)

20:18 "closed up" / "fast closed up" (Heb supports KJV)

21:15 "placed" / "cast" (Heb supports KJV)

21:22, 32 "commander" / "chief captain" (Heb supports KJV)

21:23 "here" is omitted, but rightly included in KJV, according to Heb

21:23 "posterity" / "son's son" (Heb supports NKJV)

21:25 "seized" / "violently taken away" (Heb supports KJV)

21:29 "asked" / "said" (Heb supports KJV)

22:1 "Here I am" / "behold" (Heb supports KJV)

22:8 "for Himself" / "himself" (Heb supports KJV)

22:13 "it" / "him" (Heb supports KJV)

22:14 "provided" / "seen" (Heb supports KJV)

22:17 "their" / "his" (Heb supports KJV)

23:1 "lived" / "was" (Heb supports KJV)

23:4, 9 "property" / "possession" (Heb supports KJV)

23:5 "sons" / "children" (Heb supports NKJV)

23:8 "spoke" / "communed" (Heb supports NKJV)

23:8 "wish" / "mind" (Heb supports KJV)

23:13, 16 "hearing" / "audience" (Heb supports NKJV)

23:13 "but" is omitted from NKJV, but it is in the KJV and Heb

23:17, 20 "deeded" / "made sure" (Heb supports KJV)

24:5, 6, 8 "take back" / "bring again" (Heb supports KJV)

24:8 "released" / "clear" (Heb supports KJV)

24:8 "oath" / "my oath" (Heb supports KJV)

24:10 "camels" / "camels of the camels" (Heb supports KJV)

24:14 "young woman" / "damsel" (Heb supports NKJV)

24:20 "quickly emptied" / "hasted and emptied" (Heb supports KJV)

24:21 "to know" / "to wit" (Heb supports NKJV)

24:22 "weighing half a shekel" / "of half a shekel weight" (Heb supports KJV)

24:22 "wrists"/"hands" (Heb supports KJV)

24:25 "feed" / "provender" (Heb supports NKJV)

24:27 "forsaken" / "left destitute" (Heb supports NKJV)

24:31 "place" / "room" (Heb supports NKJV)

24:41 "oath" / "my oath" (Heb supports KJV)

24:48 "way of truth" / "right way" (Heb supports NKJV)

24:51 "here" / "behold" (Heb supports KJV)

24:57 "ask her personally" / "inquire at her mouth" (Heb supports KJV)

24:60 "thou" is omitted from NKJV, although it is in the KJV and Heb

24:60 "gates" / "gate" (Heb supports KJV)

24:61 "maids" / "damsels" (Heb supports KJV)

24:62 "well" is omitted from NKJV, though it is in the KJV and Heb

24:62 "south" / "south country" (Heb supports KJV)

24:65 "who is this man?" / "what man is this?" (Heb supports KJV)

25:7 "sum" / "days" (Heb supports KJV)

25:8, 17 "breathed his last" / "gave up the ghost" (Heb supports KJV)

25:11 "Beer" / "well" (Heb supports KJV)

25:18 "east of" / "before" (Heb supports KJV)

25:21 "pleaded" / "entreated" (Heb supports KJV)

25:21 "granted his plea" / "was entreated" (Heb supports KJV)

25:22 "if all is well" / "if it be so" (Heb supports KJV)

25:23 "body" / "bowels" (Heb supports KJV)

25:28 "game" / "venison" (Heb supports NKJV)

25:33 "profit" is in KJV, but not in NKJV or Heb

25:34 "stew" / "pottage" (Heb supports KJV)

26:2 "live" / "dwell" (Heb supports KJV)

26:8 "showing endearment" / "sporting" (Heb supports KJV)

26:9 "quite obviously" / "behold of a surety" (Heb supports KJV)

26:10 "soon" / "lightly" (Heb supports KJV)

26:13 "began to prosper" / "waxed great" (Heb supports KJV)

26:13 "continued prospering" / "went forward" (Heb supports KJV)

26:14 "number" / "store" (Heb supports NKJV)

26:18 "names" / "names after the names" (Heb supports KJV)

26:20, 21, 22 "quarreled" / "strive" (Heb supports KJV)

26:26 "with" / "and" (Heb supports KJV)

26:31 "early" / "betimes" (Heb supports NKJV)

26:31 "swore an oath" / "sware" (Heb supports KJV)

26:34 "wives" / "wife" (Heb supports KJV)

27:9 "choice" / "good" (Heb supports KJV)

27:19 "told" / "badest" (Heb supports NKJV)

27:27 "surely" / "see" (Heb supports KJV)

27:29 "those who bless" / "he that blesseth" (Heb supports KJV)

27:33 "very" is omitted, though it is in the KJV and the Heb

27:33 "hunted" / "taken" (Heb supports NKJV)

27:35 "deceit" / "subtilty" (Heb supports NKJV)

27:40 "become restless" / "have dominion" (Heb supports NKJV)

27:42 "surely" / "behold" (Heb supports KJV)

28:3 "assembly" / "multitude" (Heb supports NKJV)

28:9 "in addition to" / "unto" (Heb supports KJV)

28:11 "came to" / "lighted upon" (Heb supports KJV)

28:11, 18 "his head" / "pillows" (Heb supports KJV)

28:12 "there" / "behold" (Heb supports KJV)

28:20 "made" / "vowed" (Heb supports KJV)

29:2 "saw" / "behold" (Heb supports KJV)

29:3 "would roll" / "rolled" (Heb supports KJV)

29:8 "they have rolled" / "till they roll" (Heb supports NKJV)

29:9 "was a shepherdess" / "kept them" (Heb supports KJV)

29:12, 15 "relative" / "brother" (Heb supports KJV)

29:13 "report" / "tidings" (Heb supports NKJV)

29:17 "beautiful of form and appearance" / "beautiful and well favoured" (Heb supports NKJV)

29:23 "to Jacob" / "to him" (Heb supports KJV)

29:31,33 "unloved" / "hated" (Heb supports KJV)

29:34 "attached" / "joined" (Heb supports KJV)

30:2 "aroused" / "kindled" (Heb supports KJV)

30:6 "my case" / "me" (Heb supports KJV)

30:20 "endowment" / "dowry" (Heb supports NKJV)

30:28 "name" / "appoint" (Heb supports KJV)

30:30 "great amount" / "multitude" (Heb supports KJV)

30:31 "flocks" / "flock" (Heb supports KJV)

30:32 "let me pass" / "I will pass" (Heb supports KJV)

30:33 "the subject of "/"it" (Heb supports KJV)

30:35 "speckled" / "ringstraked" (Heb supports KJV)

30:37 "almond" / "hazel" (Heb supports NKJV)

30:37, 38 "peeled" / "pilled" (Heb supports NKJV)

30:39 "flocks" is omitted from KJV, although in NKJV and Heb

30:43 "large" / "much" (Heb supports KJV)

31:1 "wealth" / "glory" (Heb supports KJV)

31:13 "made a vow" / "vowedst a vow" (Heb supports KJV)

31:18 "acquired" / "of his getting" (Heb supports NKJV)

31:20 "intended to flee" / "fled" (Heb supports KJV)

31:21 "headed" / "set his face" (Heb supports KJV)

31:21, 23, 25 "mountains" / "mount" (Heb supports KJV)

31:29 "my power" / "power of my hand" (Heb supports KJV)

31:32 "identify" / "discern" (Heb supports KJV)

31:37 "what part" / "what" (Heb supports KJV)

31:38 "miscarried" / "cast" (Heb supports NKJV)

31:42 "empty-handed" / "empty" (Heb supports KJV)

31:51 "here" / "behold" (Heb supports KJV)

32:8,11 "attacks" / "smite" (Heb supports KJV)

32:16 "successive droves" / "drove and drove" (Heb supports KJV)

32:25,32 "socket of his hip" / "hollow of his thigh" (Heb supports KJV)

32:28 "you have struggled with" / "as a prince hast thou power with" (Heb supports KJV)

32:31 "limped" / "halted" (Heb supports NKJV)

32:31, 32 "hip" / "thigh" (Heb supports KJV)

32:32 "muscle" / "sinew" (Heb supports KJV)

33:8, 12 "Esau" / "he" (Heb supports KJV)

33:8 "company" / "drove" (Heb supports NKJV)

33:13 "Jacob" / "he" (Heb supports KJV)

33:13 "nursing" / "with young" (Heb supports NKJV)

33:14 "go on ahead" / "pass over" (Heb supports KJV)

33:14 "slowly" / "softly" (Heb supports KJV)

33:14 "at a pace" / "according as" (Heb supports NKJV)

33:18 "came safely" / "came" (Heb supports KJV)

33:19 "from" / "at the hand of" (Heb supports KJV)

34:3 "strongly attracted" / "clave" (Heb supports KJV)

34:6, 8, 20 "speak" / "commune" (Heb supports NKJV)

34:19 "delay" / "deferred" (Heb supports NKJV)

34:25 "each" / "each man" (Heb supports KJV)

34:27 "had been defiled" / "they defiled" (Heb supports KJV)

34:29 "houses" / "house" (Heb supports KJV)

34:30 "obnoxious" / "to stink" (Heb supports KJV)

34:31 "treat" / "deal with" (Heb supports KJV)

35:2 "foreign" / "strange" (Heb supports NKJV)

35:2 "purify yourselves" / "be clean" (Heb supports NKJV)

35:5 "after" is in KJV and Heb, but not in NKJV

35:11 "proceed" / "shall be" (Heb supports KJV)

35:11 "body" / "loins" (Heb supports KJV)

36:6 "presence" / "face" (Heb supports KJV)

36:7 "possessions" / "riches" (Heb supports NKJV)

36:7 "too great" / "more than" (Heb supports KJV)

36:15-19 "chiefs" / "dukes" (Heb supports NKJV)

36:43 "dwelling places" / "habitations" (Heb supports NKJV)

37:2 "history" / "generations" (Heb supports KJV)

37:5 "had a dream" / "dreamed a dream" (Heb supports KJV)

37:7 "bowed down" / "made obeisance" (Heb supports NKJV)

37:14 "back" / "again" (Heb supports NKJV)

37:20, 33 "wild" / "evil" (Heb supports KJV)

37:22 "deliver" / "rid" (Heb supports NKJV)

37:25 "meal" / "bread" (Heb supports KJV)

37:25 "on their way" / "going" (Heb supports KJV)

37:27 "listened" / "were content" (Heb supports NKJV)

37:28 "traders" / "merchantmen" (Heb supports KJV)

37:28 "pulled" / "drew" (Heb supports KJV)

37:28 "him" / "Joseph" (Heb supports KJV)

37:28 "took" / "brought" (Heb supports KJV)

37:32 "do you know" / "know" (Heb supports KJV)

37:34 "waist" / "loins" (Heb supports KJV)

38:1 "departed" / "went down" (Heb supports KJV)

38:1 "visited" / "turned in" (Heb supports KJV)

38:6 "and her name" / "whose name" (Heb supports NKJV)

38:8, 9 "heir" / "seed" (Heb supports KJV)

38:14 "off" / "off from her" (Heb supports KJV)

38:18, 25 "cord" / "bracelets" (Heb supports NKJV)

38:23, 24, 29 "behold" is omitted from NKJV, but is in KJV and Heb

38:29 "unexpectedly" is added in NKJV, but missing in KJV and Heb

39:1 "from" / "of the hands" (Heb supports KJV)

39:4 "of" / "over" (Heb supports KJV)

39:4 "under his authority" / "into his hand" (Heb supports KJV)

39:5 "over" is omitted from NKJV, but is in KJV and Heb

39:6 "what" / "aught" (Heb supports KJV)

39:6 "handsome in form and appearance" / "goodly and well favoured" (Heb supports NKJV)

39:7 "longing" is added in NKJV, but missing in KJV and Heb

39:12 "ran" / "got out" (Heb supports KJV)

39:13 "outside" / "forth" (Heb supports NKJV)

39:19 "aroused" / "kindled" (Heb supports KJV)

39:20 "confined" / "bound" (Heb supports KJV)

39:23 "authority" / "hand" (Heb supports KJV)

40:2 "against" is twice omitted from NKJV, but is in KJV and Heb

40:2 "baker" / "bakers" (Heb supports KJV)

40:4 "for a while" / "continued a season" (Heb supports KJV)

40:5 "had a dream" / "dreamed a dream" (Heb supports KJV)

40:5 "its interpretation" / "according to the interpretation" (Heb supports KJV)

40:10 "its" / "her" (Heb supports KJV)

40:11, 21 "placed" / "gave" (Heb supports KJV)

40:13 "now" / "yet" (Heb supports KJV)

40:14 "get" / "bring" (Heb supports KJV)

40:19 "yet" is omitted from NKJV, but is in KJV and Heb

41:2, 5, 18, 22 "suddenly" / "behold" (Heb supports KJV)

41:2 "fine looking" / "well favoured" (Heb supports KJV)

41:2, 18 "the meadow" / "a meadow" (Heb supports KJV)

41:5, 7 "plump" / "rank" (Heb supports NKJV)

41:8 "dreams" / "dream" (Heb supports KJV)

41:11, 15 "had a dream" / "dreamed a dream" (Heb supports KJV)

41:11 "each of us" / "each man" (Heb supports KJV)

41:19 "ugliness" / "badness" (Heb supports KJV)

41:21 "would have known" / "could be known" (Heb supports KJV)

41:24 "explain" / "declare" (Heb supports KJV)

41:25, 26 "dreams" / "dream" (Heb supports KJV)

41:27 "are" / "shall be" (Heb supports KJV)

41:29 "will come" / "come" (Heb supports KJV)

41:30 "deplete" / "consume" (Heb supports KJV)

41:32 "repeated" / "doubled" (Heb supports KJV)

41:33 "select" / "look out" (Heb supports KJV)

41:35 "authority" / "hand" (Heb supports KJV)

41:36 "reserve" / "store" (Heb supports KJV)

41:37 "advice" / "thing" (Heb supports KJV)

41:40 "in regard to" is added in NKJV, but not in KJV or Heb

41:44 "your consent" / "thee" (Heb supports KJV)

41:47 "abundantly" / "by handfuls" (Heb supports KJV)

41:48 "fields" / "field" (Heb supports KJV)

41:48 "surrounded" / "round about" (Heb supports KJV)

41:49 "immeasureable" / "without number" (Heb supports KJV)

41:54 "famine" / "dearth" (Heb supports NKJV)

42:4 "calamity" / "mischief" (Heb supports KJV)

42:5 "journeyed" / "came" (Heb supports KJV)

42:6 "bowed" / "bowed themselves" (Heb supports KJV)

42:7, 8 "recognized" / "knew" (Heb supports NKJV)

42:7 "acted as a stranger" / "made himself strange" (Heb supports KJV)

42:15 "this place" / "hence" (Heb supports KJV)

42:16 "to see" is added, but not in KJV nor in Heb

42:17 "prison" / "ward" (Heb supports NKJV)

42:24 "turned away" / "turned about" (Heb supports KJV)

42:24 "talked" / "communed" (Heb supports NKJV)

42:25 "provisions" / "provision" (Heb supports KJV)

42:27 "encampment" / "inn" (Heb supports KJV)

42:27 "saw" / "espied" (Heb supports NKJV)

42:28 "has been restored" / "is restored" (Heb supports NKJV)

42:28 "were afraid" / "heart failed" (Heb supports KJV)

42:36 "want to" is added in NKJV, but not in KJV nor in Heb

42:37 "hands" / "hand" (Heb supports KJV)

42:38 "hair" / "hairs" (Heb supports NKJV)

43:7 "possibly" / "certainly" (Heb supports KJV)

43:9 "I myself" / "I" (Heb supports KJV)

43:11 "then" / "now" (Heb supports KJV)

43:11 "some" is added in NKJV, but not in KJV or Heb

43:11 "pistachio nuts" / "nuts" (Heb supports NKJV)

43:16 "slaughter an animal" / "slay" (Heb supports NKJV)

43:18 "seize" / "fall upon" (Heb supports KJV)

43:22 "do not know" / "cannot tell" (Heb supports NKJV)

43:26 "bowed down" / "bowed themselves" (Heb supports KJV)

43:27 "well-being" / "welfare" (Heb supports KJV)

43:28 "prostrated themselves" / "made obeisance" (Heb supports NKJV)

43:30 "heart" / "bowels" (Heb supports KJV)

43:31 "serve" / "set" (Heb supports KJV)

43:32 "set a place" / "set" (Heb supports KJV)

43:32 "food" / "bread" (Heb supports KJV)

43:33 "looked in astonishment" / "marvelled" (Heb supports KJV)

44:3 "dawned" / "was light" (Heb supports KJV)

44:4 "get up" / "up" (Heb supports NKJV)

44:7 "according to" is omitted from NKJV, but in KJV and Heb

44:18 "hearing" / "ears" (Heb supports KJV)

44:20 "children" is added in NKJV, but not in KJV or in Heb

44:29 "calamity" / "mischief" (Heb supports KJV)

44:29, 31 "hair" / "hairs" (Heb supports NKJV)

44:34 "if" / "and" (Heb supports KJV)

45:11 "provide for" / "nourish" (Heb supports KJV)

45:18, 20 "best" / "good" (Heb supports KJV)

45:22 "provisions" / "provision" (Heb supports KJV)

45:23 "food" / "meat" (Heb supports NKJV)

45:24 "become troubled" / "fall out" (Heb supports NKJV)

45:27 "but when" / "and" (Heb supports KJV)

46:7 "with him" is omitted from NKJV, but in KJV and Heb

46:15, 18, 22, 25, 26, 27 "persons" / "souls" (Heb supports KJV)

46:23 "son" / "sons" (Heb supports KJV)

46:26 "body" / "loins" (Heb supports KJV)

46:28 "point out before him" / "direct his face" (Heb supports KJV)

46:31 "those of" is added in NKJV, but not in KJV or Heb

47:6 "chief herdsmen" / "rulers" (Heb supports KJV)

47:12 "provided" / "nourished" (Heb supports KJV)

47:16 "is gone" / "fail" (Heb supports KJV)

47:18 "next" / "second" (Heb supports KJV)

47:22 "rations" / "portion" (Heb supports KJV)

47:24 "harvest" / "increase" (Heb supports KJV)

47:30 "let me" / "I will" (Heb supports KJV)

48:2 "and said" is omitted from NKJV, but in KJV and Heb

48:7 "distance" / "way" (Heb supports NKJV)

48:11 "in fact" / "lo" (Heb supports KJV)

48:12 "brought" / "brought out" (Heb supports KJV)

48:12 "bowed down" / "bowed himself" (Heb supports KJV)

48:20 "thus" is added in NKJV, but not in KJV or Heb

49:6 "let enter" / "come" (Heb supports KJV)

49:6 "let be united" / "be united" (Heb supports KJV)

49:6 "hamstrung an ox" / "digged down a wall" (Heb supports NKJV, based on vowel pointing)

49:9 "bows" / "stooped" (Heb supports NKJV)

49:9, 14 "lies down" / "couched" (Heb supports NKJV)

49:9 "lion" / "old lion" (Heb supports NKJV)

49:10 "obedience" / "gathering" (Heb supports NKJV)

49:13 "shall adjoin" / "unto" (Heb supports KJV)

49:15 "band of slaves" / "servant unto tribute" (Heb supports KJV)

49:17 "viper" / "adder" (Heb supports KJV)

49:19 "tramp upon" / "overcome" (Heb supports KJV)

49:21 "uses" / "giveth" (Heb supports KJV)

49:23 "bitterly" / "sorely" (Heb supports NKJV)

49:26 "excelled" / "prevailed" (Heb supports KJV)

49:27 "ravenous" / "shall ravin" (Heb supports KJV)

49:33 "drew up" / "gathered" (Heb supports KJV)

49:33 "breathed his last" / "yielded up the ghost" (Heb supports KJV)

50:3 "required" / "fulfilled" (Heb supports KJ

50:4 "hearing" / "ears" (Heb supports KJV)

50:8 "as well as" / "and" (Heb supports KJV)

50:9 "gathering" / "company" (Heb supports KJV)

50:15 "may actually repay" / "will certainly requite" (Heb supports KJV)

50:21 "provide" / "nourish" (Heb supports KJV)

Summary:

1. 86 times the Heb supports NKJV.

2. 322 times the Heb supports KJV.

3. Thus, out of 408 discrepancies, the KJV is preferable 79% of the time, despite the "antiquated" words.

4. Eliminating the "antiquated" words, the KJV is preferable 88% of the time.

Appendix B

Differences between NKJV/KJV in Romans

(There are 4,325 words in KJV for Romans)

In the following analysis, the NKJV rendering in each verse appears first, separated from the KJV by /, and the comment that follows reflects research from Greek lexicons (Vine, Thayer, and BAG). Gk is an abbreviation for the Greek language.

1:10 "find a way" / "have a prosperous journey" (Gk supports KJV)

1:13 "want you to be unaware" / "have you ignorant" (Gk supports KJV)

1:13 "planned" / "purposed" (Gk supports KJV)

1:13 "hindered" / "let" (Gk supports NKJV)

1:14 "the" is added four times in KJV, but not in NKJV or Gk

1:21 "thoughts" / "imaginations" (Gk supports NKJV)

1:21 "hearts" / "heart" (Gk supports KJV)

1:22 "professing" / "professing themselves" (Gk supports NKJV)

1:25, 26 "exchanged for" / "changed into" (Gk supports KJV)

1:25 "the lie" / "a lie" (Gk supports NKJV)

1:25 "rather than" / "more than" (Gk supports NKJV)

1:27 "committing" / "working" (Gk supports KJV)

1:27 "penalty" / "recompense" (Gk supports KJV)

1:28 "debased" / "reprobate" (Gk supports KJV)

1:28 "fitting" / "convenient" (Gk supports NKJV)

1:29 "strife" / "debate" (Gk supports NKJV)

1:29 "evil-mindedness" / "malignity" (Gk supports KJV)

1:30 "violent" / "despiteful" (Gk supports KJV)

1:31 "undiscerning" / "without understanding" (Gk supports KJV)

1:31 "untrustworthy" / "covenantbreakers" (Gk supports KJV)

1:32 "deserving" / "worthy" (Gk supports KJV)

1:32 "approve of" / "have pleasure in" (Gk supports KJV)

2:2 "know" / "are sure" (Gk supports NKJV)

2:5 "in accordance with" / "after" (Gk supports NKJV)

2:5 "in" / "against" (Gk supports NKJV)

2:6, 10 "each one" / "every man" (Gk supports NKJV)

2:13 "in the sight of" / "before" (Gk supports KJV)

2:14 "in" / "contained in" (Gk supports NKJV)

2:14 "although" is added in NKJV, but not in KJV or Gk

2:17 "indeed" / "behold" (Gk supports KJV)

2:20 "having" / "which hast" (Gk supports NKJV)

2:25 "is profitable" / "profiteth" (Gk supports KJV)

2:26 "an uncircumcised man" / "the uncircumcision" (Gk supports KJV)

2:26 "righteous requirements" / "righteousness" (Gk supports KJV)

2:27 "written code" / "letter" (Gk supports KJV)

2:27 "are a transgressor" / "does transgress" (Gk supports NKJV)

3:2 "that" is omitted in NKJV, but is in KJV and Gk

3:7 "increased" / "abounded" (Gk supports KJV)

3:8 "their" / "whose" (Gk supports KJV)

3:9 "previously charged" / "proved before" (Gk supports NKJV)

3:12 "turned aside" / "gone out of the way" (Gk supports NKJV)

3:13 "practiced" / "used" (Gk supports KJV)

3:21 "revealed" / "manifested" (Gk supports KJV)

3:22 "in" / "of" (Gk supports KJV)

3:25, 26 "demonstrate" / "declare" (Gk supports NKJV)

3:25 "by His blood, through faith" / "through faith in his blood" (Gk supports KJV) This makes His blood the object of faith.

3:25 "in his forbearance God had" / "through the forbearance of God" (Gk supports KJV)

3:29, 6:3 "or" is omitted in KJV, but is in NKJV and Gk

3:29 "the God" is added in NKJV, but not in KJV or Gk

3:30 "since" / "seeing" (Gk supports NKJV)

4:1 "according to" / "pertaining to" (Gk supports NKJV)

4:10 "circumcised" / "in circumcision" (Gk supports KJV)

4:10 "uncircumcised" / "in uncircumcision" (Gk supports KJV)

4:10 "while" / "in" (Gk supports KJV)

4:16 "according to" / "by" (Gk supports NKJV)

4:17 "in the presence of" / "before" (Gk supports KJV)

4:17 "exist" / "be" (Gk supports KJV)

4:18 "descendants" / "seed" (Gk supports KJV)

4:19 "and" / "neither yet" (Gk supports NKJV)

4:24 "to us" / "to whom" (Gk supports KJV)

4:24 "who believe" / "if we believe" (Gk supports NKJV)

5:3 "produces" / "worketh" (Gk supports KJV)

5:4 "character" / "experience" (Gk supports NKJV)

5:5 "disappoint" / "maketh ashamed" (Gk supports KJV)

5:5 "has been poured out" / "is shed abroad" (Gk supports NKJV)

5:11 "reconciliation" / "atonement" (Gk supports NKJV)

5:18 "one man's" / "of one" (Gk supports KJV)

5:18 "resulting in" / "to" (Gk supports KJV)

5:19 "also" is omitted in KJV, but in NKJV and Gk

5:19 "man" is added in NKJV, but not in KJV or Gk

6:2 "died" / "are dead" (Gk supports NKJV)

6:7 "has been freed" / "is freed" (Gk supports NKJV)

6:9 "having been raised" / "being raised" (Gk supports KJV)

6:13 "present" / "yield" (Gk supports NKJV)

6:13 "being alive" / "those that are alive" (Gk supports NKJV)

6:16 "you are that one's slave" / "his servants ye are" (Gk supports KJV)

6:17 "to which you were delivered" / "which was delivered you" (Gk supports NKJV)

7:5 "passions" / "motions" (Gk supports NKJV)

7:5 "aroused" is added in NKJV, but not in KJV or in Gk

7:6 "to what" / "wherein" (Gk supports KJV)

7:7 "covetousness" / "lust" (Gk supports KJV)

7:9 "for" is omitted in NKJV, but in KJV and Gk

7:15 "understand" / "allow" (Gk supports NKJV)

7:24 "this body of death" / "the body of this death" (Gk supports KJV)

8:1 "according to" / "after" (Gk supports NKJV)

8:3 "by sending" / "sending" (Gk supports KJV)

8:4 "righteous requirement" / "righteousness" (Gk supports KJV)

8:5 "set their minds on" / "mind" (Gk supports KJV)

8:13 "put to death" / "mortify" (Gk supports KJV)

8:22 "labors with birth pangs" / "travaileth in pain" (Gk supports KJV)

8:33 "bring a charge against" / "lay anything to the charge" (Gk supports NKJV)

8:34 "and furthermore" / "yea rather" (Gk supports KJV)

8:34 "also risen" / "risen again" (Gk supports NKJV)

9:2 "sorrow" / "heaviness" (Gk supports NKJV)

9:4 "and" is omitted 4 times in NKJV, but is in KJV and Gk

9:17 "very purpose" / "same purpose" (Gk supports KJV)

9:20 "but indeed" / "nay" (Gk supports KJV)

10:3 "seeking" / "going about" (Gk supports NKJV)

10:5 "writes" / "describeth" (Gk supports NKJV)

10:6 "which" is added in KJV, but not in NKJV or in Gk

11:2 "do you not know" / "wot ye not" (Gk supports NKJV)

11:2 "pleads" / "maketh intercession" (Gk supports KJV)

11:3 "torn down" / "digged down" (Gk supports KJV)

11:4 "divine response" / "answer of God" (Gk supports NKJV)

11:5 "also" is omitted in NKJV, but is in KJV and Gk

11:6 "then" is added in KJV, but not in NKJV or in Gk

11:8 "stupor" / "slumber" (Gk supports NKJV)

11:9 "become" / "be made" (Gk supports KJV)

11:12 "failure" / "diminishing" (Gk supports KJV)

11:14 "jealousy" / "emulation" (Gk supports NKJV)

11:15 "their being cast away" / "casting away of them" (Gk supports KJV)

11:15 "acceptance" / "receiving" (Gk supports KJV)

11:17 "become a partaker" / "partakest" (Gk supports NKJV)

11:18 "supports" is added in NKJV, but is not in KJV or Gk

11:21 "He may not spare" / "lest he also spare not" (Gk supports KJV)

11:22 "consider" / "behold" (Gk supports KJV)

11:24 "cultivated" / "good" (Gk supports NKJV)

11:31 "the mercy shown" / "your mercy" (Gk supports KJV)

11:35 "repaid" / "recompensed" (Gk supports NKJV)

12:3 "each one" / "every man" (Gk supports NKJV)

12:4 "function" / "office" (Gk supports NKJV)

12:5 "individually" / "every one" (Gk supports KJV)

12:6 "according to" is omitted in NKJV, but is in KJV and Gk

12:8 "liberality" / "simplicity" (Gk supports KJV)

12:9 "hypocrisy" / "dissimulation" (Gk supports NKJV)

12:10 "giving preference" / "preferring" (Gk supports KJV)

12:11 "lagging" / "slothful" (Gk supports KJV)

12:11 "diligence" / "business" (Gk supports NKJV)

12:16 "associate with" / "condescend to" (Gk supports NKJV)

12:16 "good" / "honest" (Gk supports NKJV)

12:18 "depends upon" / "lieth in" (Gk supports KJV)

13:1 "governing authorities" / "higher powers" (Gk supports KJV)

13:1 "exist" / "be" (Gk supports KJV)

13:2 "bring" / "receive" (Gk supports KJV)

13:2; 14:23 "judgment" / "damnation" (Gk supports NKJV)

13:9 "the commandments" is added in NKJV, but not in KJV or Gk

13:9 "summed up" / "comprehended" (Gk supports NKJV)

13:13 "lust" / "wantonness" (Gk supports NKJV)

13:15 "put on" / "put ye on" (Gk supports KJV)

14:1 "disputes over doubtful things" / "doubtful disputations" (Gk supports KJV)

14:2 "another" is added in KJV, but not in NKJV or in Gk

14:13 "resolve" / "judge" (Gk supports KJV)

14:13 "not to put" / "that no man put" (Gk supports NKJV)

14:15, 17 "food" / "meat" (Gk supports NKJV)

14:15 "no longer" / "now" (Gk supports NKJV)

14:22 "approves" / "alloweth" (Gk supports NKJV)

15:2 "leading" is added in NKJV, but not in KJV or Gk

15:8 "has become" / "was" (Gk supports NKJV)

15:11 "peoples" / "people" (Gk supports NKJV)

15:17 "reason to" is added in NKJV, but not in KJV or Gk

15:21 "announced" / "spoken" (Gk supports NKJV)

15:24 "enjoy" / "filled" (Gk supports KJV)

15:24 "for awhile" is added in NKJV, but not in KJV or Gk

15:27 "material" / "carnal" (Gk supports KJV)

15:29 "I know" / "I am sure" (Gk supports NKJV)

16:1 "which" is omitted in NKJV, but is in KJV and Gk

16:2 "in a manner worthy" / "as becometh" (Gk supports NKJV)

16:2 "helper" / "succourer" (Gk supports NKJV)

16:17 "urge" / "beseech" (Gk supports NKJV)

16:17 "note" / "mark" (Gk supports KJV)

16:18 "smooth" / "good" (Gk supports NKJV)

16:19 "become known" / "come abroad" (Gk supports KJV)

16:23 "treasurer" / "chamberlain" (Gk supports NKJV)

Summary:

1. There are 163 discrepancies between the two versions.

2. Of these, 91 times the Greek supported the KJV, and 72 times it supported the NKJV.

3. Thus, 56% of the time, the KJV is superior, despite the fact that many of the cases where NKJV is preferred are due to antiquated English words.

4. If adjustments are made for "antiquated" English terminology, the percentages change to 63% in agreement with KJV and 37% in favor of NKJV.

Appendix C

Differences between NKJV/KJV in Revelation

(There are 6,165 words in KJV in Revelation.)

In the following analysis, the NKJV rendering in each verse appears first, separated from the KJV by /, and the comment that follows reflects research from Greek lexicons (Vine, Thayer, and BAG). Gk is an abbreviation for the Greek language

1:13 "band" / "girdle" (Gk supports KJV)

2:3 "have persevered" / "have borne" (Gk supports KJV)

2:10 "indeed" / "behold" (Gk supports KJV, also in 2:22; 3:9)

2:22 "sick bed" / "bed" (context supports KJV)

3:5 NKJV omits "the same," which is in KJV and Gk

3:10 "command to persevere" / "word of patience" (Gk supports KJV)

3:18 "may not be revealed" / "do not appear" (Gk supports NKJV)

4:1 "door standing open" / "door was opened" (GK supports KJV)

4:3 "in appearance" / "to look upon" (Gk supports NKJV)

4:8 "eyes around and within" / "wings about . . . eyes within" (GK supports NKJV)

4:11 "by your will" / "for thy pleasure" (Gk supports NKJV)

5:3 "or" / "neither" (Gk supports KJV)

5:8 "bowls" / "vials" (Gk supports NKJV)

6:2 NKJV omits "and" before "he that sat," but it is in Gk and KJV

6:5 NKJV omits the first "and," but it is in Gk and KJV

6:6 "quart of wheat" / "measure of wheat" (GK supports KJV, twice in this verse)

6:9 NKJV omits the first "and," but it is in Gk and KJV

6:10 "until You judge" / "dost thou not judge\" (Gk supports KJV)

6:11 "a little while longer" / "a little season" (Gk supports KJV)

6:13 "drops its late figs" / "casteth her untimely figs" (Gk supports KJV)

6:14 "sky receded" / "heaven departed" (Gk supports KJV)

7:1 NKJV omits "and" at the beginning of the verse, but it is in Gk and KJV

7:9 "standing" / "stood" (Gk supports NKJV)

7:9 "palm branches" / "palms" (Gk supports KJV)

7:10 "salvation belongs to" / "salvation to" (Gk supports KJV)

8:1 NKJV omits "and" at the beginning of the verse, but it is in Gk and KJV

8:5 NKJV omits the second "and" in this verse, but it is in Gk and KJV

8:11 NKJV omits "called" before "Wormwood," but it is in GK and KJV

8:13 "blasts" / "voices" (Gk Supports KJV)

9:4 "they were commanded" / "it was commanded them" (Gk supports KJV)

9:5 "they were not given authority to kill" / "to them it was given that they should not kill" (Gk supports KJV)

9:7 "something like" is added in NKJV, but not in Gk or KJV

9:8, 10 NKJV omits "and", but it is in Gk and KJV

9:16 "now" / "and" (Gk supports KJV)

9:17 "fiery red" / "fire" (Gk supports KJV)

9:17 "hyacinth blue" / "jacinth" (Gk supports KJV)

9:17 "sulphur yellow" / "brimstone" (Gk supports KJV)

9:19 "harmed" / "hurt" (Gk supports NKJV)

9:20 "yet" is omitted in NKJV, but is in Gk and KJV

10:1 "and" is omitted in NKJV, but is in Gk and KJV

10:1 "still" is added in NKJV, but is not in Gk or KJV

10:2 "and" is omitted in NKJV, but is in Gk and KJV

10:5 "and" is omitted in NKJV, but is in Gk and KJV

10:9 "eat it" / "eat it up" (Gk supports KJV)

11:1 "measuring rod" / "rod" (Gk supports KJV)

11:17 "to thee" is added in KJV, but not in Gk or NKJV

11:18 "reward" / "give reward" (Gk supports KJV)

12:1 "now" / "and" (Gk supports KJV)

12:1 "with" / "and" (Gk supports KJV)

12:1 "garland" / "crown" (Gk supports KJV)

12:3 "fiery red" / "red" (Gk supports KJV)

12:7 "war broke out" / "there was war" (Gk supports KJV)

12:15, 16 "spewed" / "cast" (Gk supports KJV)

13:1 "rising" / "rise" (Gk supports NKJV)

13:1 "blasphemous name" / "name of blasphemy" (Gk supports KJV)

13:14, 15 "granted" / "had power" (Gk supports NKJV)

14:4 "these are the ones" / "these are they" (Gk supports NKJV)

14:10 "full strength" / "without mixture" (Gk supports KJV)

15:4 "have been manifested" / "were made manifest" (Gk supports KJV)

15:6 "bands" / "girdles" (Gk supports KJV)

15:7 "bowls / "vials" (Gk supports NKJV)

15:8 "into" is omitted in NKJV, but is in Gk and KJV

16:1 "go" / "go your ways" (Gk supports KJV)

16:1, 2, 3, 4, 8, 10, 12, 17 "bowl" / "vial" (Gk supports NKJV)

16:3 "creature" / "soul" (Gk supports KJV)

16:6 "it is their just due" / "they are worthy" (Gk supports KJV)

16:16 "they gathered" / "he gathered" (Gk supports KJV)

16:19 "now" / "and" (Gk supports KJV)

16:21 "that plague" / "the plague" (Gk supports KJV)

17:4 "adorned" / "decked" (Gk supports NKJV)

17:6 "amazement" / "admiration" (Gk supports NKJV)

17:11, 12 the first "and" is omitted in NKJV, but is in Gk and KJV

18:6 "repay her double" / "double unto her double" (Gk supports KJV)

18:7 "in the measure" / "how much" (Gk supports KJV)

18:7 "in the same measure" / "so much" (Gk supports KJV)

18:13 "cattle" / "beasts" (Gk supports NKJV)

18:16 "adorned" / "decked" (Gk supports NKJV)

18:17 "all who travel" / "all the company" (Gk supports KJV)

18:19 "wealth" / "costliness" (Gk supports KJV)

19:2 "on her" / "at her hand" (Gk supports KJV)

19:3 "rises up" / "rose up" (Gk supports NKJV)

19:11 "now" / "and" (Gk supports KJV)

19:20 "two" / "both" (Gk supports NKJV)

20:2 "serpent of old" / "old serpent" (Gk supports KJV)

20:7 "now" / "and" (Gk supports KJV)

20:13 "his works" / "their works" (Gk supports KJV)

21:1 "Now" / "And" (Gk supports KJV)

21:4 "There shall be no more" / "neither shall there be anymore" (Gk supports KJV)

21:8 "cowardly" / "fearful" (Gk supports KJV)

21:9 "bowls" / "vials" (Gk supports NKJV)

21:14 "Now" / "And" (Gk supports KJV)

21:18 "And" is in the Gk and KJV, but not in NKJV

21:18 "construction" / "building" (Gk supports KJV)

21:21 "individual" / "several" (Gk supports NKJV)

21:27 "into" is in Gk and KJV, but omitted in NKJV

22:2 "yielded" / "yielding" (Gk supports NKJV)

22:2 "her" is in Gk and KJV, but omitted in NKJV

22:12 "according to his work" / "according as his work shall be" (Gk supports KJV)

22:15 "But" / "For" (Gk supports NKJV)

22:15 "practices" / "maketh" (Gk supports KJV)

Summary:

Out of 100 discrepancies found, KJV is superior in 77 places (77%).

Endnotes

[1] James B. Williams and Randolph Shayler, eds., God's Word in Our Hands, (Greenville, SC: Ambassador Emerald International, 2003), 336.

[2] Ibid., 336.

[3] Posted on January 30, 2011 by admin (www.vulgate.net).

[4] R. Laird Harris, Gleason L. Archer, and Bruce K. Waltke, eds., Theological Wordbook of the Old Testament, (Chicago: Moody Press, 1980), Vol 1, 53.

[5] Brooke Foss Westcott and Fenton John Anthony Hort, The New Testament in the Original Greek (New York: The Macmillan Company, 1928), 563.

[6] Erwin Nestle and Kurt Aland, eds., Novum Testamentum Graece (Stuttgart, Germany: Wurttembergischen Bibelenstalt Stuttgart, 24th edition, 1960), 60.

[7] Kurt Aland, Matthew Black, Bruce M. Metzger, and Allen Wikgren, editors, The Greek New Testament (Stuttgart: Wurttemberg Bible Society, 1966), vi.

[8] Ibid., vii.

[9] Ibid., x.

[10] Ibid., x.

[11] Ibid., x-xi.

[12] Clayton Harrop, History of the New Testament in Plain Language, (Waco: Word Books, 1984), 81-82.

[13] Ibid., 104.

[14] Roy T. Beacham & Kevin T. Bauder, eds., <u>One Bible Only?,</u> (Grand Rapids: Kregel Publications, 2001), 21.

[15] Ibid, 59.

[16] The Faculty of Central Baptist Theological Seminary, <u>The Bible Version Debate: The Perspective of Central Baptist Theological Seminary</u>, (Minneapolis: Central Baptist Theological Seminary, 1997), 98.

[17] Ibid., 80.

[18] Rolland McCune, <u>Promise Unfulfilled</u>, (Greenville: Ambassador International, 2004), 161.

[19] William L. Lumpkin, <u>Baptist Confessions of Faith</u>, (Valley Forge: Judson Press, 1969), 44.

[20] Ibid., 82.

[21] Ibid., 117.

[22] Ibid., 131.

[23] Ibid., 66.

[24] Ibid., 70.

[25] Ibid., 251.

[26] Ibid., 253.

[27] Ibid., 299.

[28] Ibid., 325.

[29] www.spurgeon.org/~phil/creeds/phila.htm#2

[30] Lumpkin, Ibid., 361-362.

[31] Kurt Aland, Ibid., VII, 733.

[32] Joseph Henry Thayer, ed., A Greek-English Lexicon of the New Testament, (Edinburgh: T. & T. Clark, 1955), 591.

[33] Gerhard Kittel, ed., Δ-Η, Vol II of Theological Dictionary of the New Testament (Grand Rapids: Wm. B. Eerdmans Publishing Company, 1964), 364.

[34] Rolland McCune, Ibid.,75.

[35] Nestle, Ibid., 68-69.

[36] Daniel B. Wallace, "The Majority Text Theory: History, Methods and Critique," Journal of the Evangelical Theological Society (20 November 1993), 20.

[37] Archibald Thomas Robertson, The Gospel According to Mark, Vol I of Word Pictures in the New Testament, (Nashville: Broadman Press, 1930), 402.

[38] The New International Version of the New Testament, (Grand Rapids: Zondervan Bible Publishers, 1980), 121.

[39] Clayton Harrop, Ibid., 91.

[40] Donald L. Brake, A Visual History of the King James Bible, (Grand Rapids: Baker Books, 2011), 265.

[41] Ibid., 150.

[42] Alexander Roberts and James Donaldson, eds., The Apostolic Fathers

with Justin Martyr and Irenaeus , Vol I of The Ante-Nicene Fathers, (Grand Rapids: Wm. B. Eerdmans Publishing Company, 1956), 2.

[43] Ibid., 13, footnote 5.

[44] Ibid., footnote 13.

[45] Ibid., 14, footnote 6.

[46] Ibid., footnote 12.

[47] Ibid., 15, footnote 14.

[48] Ibid., 25, footnote 8.

[49] Ibid., 26, footnote 1.

[50] Ibid., 26, footnote 2.

[51] Ibid., 27, footnote 18.

[52] Ibid., 28, footnote 6.

[53] Ibid., 28, footnote 9.

[54] Ibid., footnote 1.

[55] Ibid., 30, footnote 4.

[56] Edward Miller in the Preface to John William Burgon, The Traditional Text, (Collingswood, NJ: reprinted by The Bible for Today, 1983), x.

[57] www.en.wikipedia.org/wiki/Vetus_Latina.

[58] www.drbo.org.

[59] www.speedbible.com.

[60] www.vulgate.net.

[61] www.bombaxo.com/jerome.html.

[62] Ibid.

[63] Kurt Aland, The Text of the New Testament: An Introduction to the Critical Editions and to the Theory and Practice of Modern Textual Criticism, (Grand Rapids: Wm. B. Eerdmans Publishing Co., 1995), 181-210.

[64] www.peshitta.info/gospel/mark_16.htm.

[65] www.blessedquietness.com/journal/housechu/jerome-preface-first-john-5-7.htm.

[66] www.cranfordville.com.

[67] Beacham, Ibid., 58.

[68] Harris, Ibid., Vol 2, 757.

[69] James B.Williams, Ibid., 341.

[70] Augustus Hopkins Strong, Systematic Theology: Three Volumes in One, (Philadelphia: Judson Press, 1907), 198.

[71] Ibid., 198-199.

[72] Rolland McCune, Ibid, 173.

[73] W. Edward Glenny, The Bible Version Debate: The Perspective of Central Baptist Theological Seminary, (Minneapolis: Central Baptist Theological Seminary, 1997), 84.

74 Charles L. Surrett, Which Greek Text?, (Kings Mountain, NC: Surrett Family Publications, 1999), 50-51.

75 Thomas M. Strouse, "Psalm 12:6-7 and the Permanent Preservation of God's Words," essay published by Emmanuel Baptist Seminary, Newington, CT (November 2001), 4-5.

76 Daniel B. Wallace, Ibid., 13.

77 Ibid.

78 Ibid., 14.

79 Ibid., 19.

80 Ibid., 16.

81 Ibid., 20.

82 Clayton Harrop, Ibid., 80.

83 Roy T. Beacham, Ibid., 23-26.

84 Ibid., 23.

85 James B. Williams, Ibid., 342.

86 Harris, Ibid., 701.

87 Clayton Harrop, Ibid., 68.

88 Erwin Nestle, Ibid., 59.

89 George Eldon Ladd, The New Testament and Criticism, (Grand Rapids: William B. Eerdmans Publishing Company, 1983), 71.

90 Ibid., 216.

[91] Wallace, Ibid., 14-19.

[92] Clayton Harrop, Ibid., 28.

[93] Ibid., 68-69.

[94] www.bible-researcher.com.

[95] Westcott, Ibid., 548.

[96] Ibid., 573.

[97] Ibid., 563.

[98] Ibid., 556.

[99] Ibid., 555.

[100] Clayton Harrop, Ibid., 44.

[101] Westcott, Ibid., 562.

[102] Donald L. Brake, <u>A Visual History of the King James Bible</u>, (Grand Rapids: Baker Books, 2011), 135.

[103] Ibid., 136.

[104] Ibid., 139.

[105] Ibid., 139.

[106] Ibid., 136.

[107] Ibid., 137.

[108] Arthur L. Farstad, <u>The New King James Version: In the Great Tradition</u>, (Nashville: Thomas Nelson Publishers, 1989).

---

[109] Ibid., 3.

[110] Ibid., 129-140.

[111] Ibid., 7.

[112] Daniel B. Wallace, Ibid., 13.

www.ingramcontent.com/pod-product-compliance
Lightning Source LLC
Chambersburg PA
CBHW070502100426
42743CB00010B/1728